The Bo-Tree at Bodh-Gayā.

The Life and Work of BUDDHAGHOSHA

Bimala Charan Law

LOW PRICE PUBLICATIONS
Delhi-110052

Distributed by
D.K. Publishers Distributors (P) Ltd.
4834/24, Ansari Road, Darya Ganj,
New Delhi-110002
Phones: 51562573, 51562574, 51562575
e-mail: dkpd@del3.vsnl.net.in
url: www.dkpd.com

First Published 1923

Reprinted in **LPP** 2005

ISBN 81-7536-387-8

Published by
Low Price Publications
A-6, Nimri Commercial Centre,
Near Ashok Vihar Phase-IV,
Delhi-110052
Phones: 27452453
e-mail: lpp@nde.vsnl.net.in
url: www.lppindia.com

Printed at
D K Fine Art Press P Ltd.
Delhi-110052

PRINTED IN INDIA

CALCUTTA ORIENTAL SERIES
No. 9.E.3.

THE LIFE AND WORK OF BUDDHAGHOSA

BY

BIMALA CHARAN LAW, M.A., B.L.

Author, Ksatriya Clans in Buddhist India, Historical Gleanings, etc.

WITH A FOREWORD BY

MRS. C. A. F. RHYS DAVIDS, D.LITT., M.A.

Fellow of University College, London. Author, A Buddhist Manual of Psychological Ethics, Buddhist Psychology, Buddhism, Psalms of the Early Buddhists, Dialogues of the Buddha, etc., etc.

CALCUTTA AND SIMLA

THACKER, SPINK & CO

1923

TO MY TEACHERS AND FRIENDS.

FOREWORD

I SET down here at the author's request a few words of introduction to his book on Buddhaghosa and his works. But Mr. Bimala Charan Law as an investigator in that unharvested field, needs no introduction. By me lies his prolegomenon to it, published over two years ago, in the Journal of the Asiatic Society of Bengal. In that essay, he drew up a list of 14 questions on his present subject. All were of historical interest. All would have to be discussed in any critical history of Buddhaghosa's work. He had there no scope to deal with any one of them. Here the titles of his chapters taken together virtually cover those 14 questions.

His book will be by no means a last word on the subject. It will be relatively easy for European scholars, less undaunted than Mr. Law, to carry forward their work when we get all that has been ascribed to Buddhaghosa printed in Roman letter. But the book is all the more needed now as a very useful compendium of what we yet know of Buddhaghosa, both from his own works and from other documents. Theories about the great commentator are cropping up. They rest on a more or less slender basis of evidence from lack of more historical prolegomena such as this book affords. We have recently assisted in publishing Mr. Nagai's theory that "the Visuddhi-magga is in reality a revised version of Upatissa's Vimutti-magga." (J.P.T.S., 1917–19, p. 80.) And M. Louis Finot has lately drawn attention to the plausibility of the conclusion, that in 'Buddhaghosa' we may have no historical man, but a myth of the name, a myth of 'Buddha-vacana,' on which are fathered the works usually ascribed to the person who was the contemporary of Buddhadatta. The disciple, it would seem, is to undergo, for a time, a fate analogous to that which befel his Master. Mr. Law has gone deeper into the works ascribed to Buddhaghosa than any other English-writing author; he has gone deeper into the works referring to Buddhaghosa than most men. And for him, the great commentator is still a historically real man, teaching and writing in the fifth century A.D. in Ceylon, as he may now be teaching and writing, it may be on earth, it may be in another world.

Here I have but one point of contributory matter to make. The title of Chapter VIII in this book, as sent me by Mr. Law, is entitled 'Interpretation of Buddhism.' There is so much in this word 'Buddhism' to interpret. In my Buddhist Psychology (Quest Series, London, 1914, Ch. IX), I made the attempt to set down a few instances where Buddhaghosa was the spokesman of interesting developments in Buddhist psychological ideas. I also dragged in instances of equally interesting philosophical growth, such as the attempt to analyse the nature of relation in terms of causality. Since that year I have had the privilege of preparing a provisional edition of the Visuddhi-magga for European readers. (To have edited a work from existing Asiatic editions is a little matter; to have been the first to get it into Roman letter is a high privilege). This has naturally left me a little less ignorant than before. I noted that Buddhaghosa referred often—21 times to a certain academic tradition which he calls *Porāṇā* and *Porāṇakathā*—the 'talk,' or 'teaching of the Men of Old'—a number of views metrically expressed. And he follows that tradition, at least, where he quotes it. Just as he clinches a doctrine by falling back on the word of the Exalted One in the Suttanta, so elsewhere it is enough for him to call in those Men of Old and say 'as the *Porāṇas* said.'

These *Porāṇas* were not included among the Canonical compilers, or they would be quoted as such. They appear to have been of later date. They are the 'Fathers' of the Theravāda Sāsana. They represent, in so far as they speak philosophically, the philosophy built up on the simpler archaically expressed teachings of the Suttas. They were cultured men according to the light of their day. But they were working along a line of thinking that was 'orthodox,' and therefore no longer free. And they do not represent the missionary mood of the Sutta teachers, anxious above all things to 'save souls.' They were the bookmen, the academicians, the cloistered scribes of the new predominant 'Buddhist' culture. And they were doing good work in an orphaned church. It is no small matter to be wise leaders in any cult. It is a great matter to be wise in a cult which had, by the teaching of its Great Founder, cut itself adrift from doctrines and beliefs that form the support of every other religion. After all, do any after-born teachers hand on unalloyed the truths revealed to and by an inspired Helper of men? They are concerned to be not so much creative, as explicative, and interpretative. Thus diverted, their mental energy outpaces their knowledge and forces their logic. So these 'Fathers' pondered on fundamental tenets such as Anicca, Anatta, on the deliberate reservations and silences of the Founder concerning the First and Last things of Life, on a Dhamma revealed by a man which should replace for a while the faiths in debased theologies and animisms, and foster the 'Divine Life' (Brahmachariya) between man and man. So pondering they improved, or thought they improved, on the man's simpler teaching. By a logic of Anicca and Anatta, and an ignorance of how life survives, they denied (as he did not) that there was 'a going on, a running on' of the person from one world to another at death. They denied (as he did not) that sentient life or saṁsāra was ever initiated by Deity.

I see that Mr. Law has not anticipated me on this point (I have touched on it in the Afterword to the Visuddhimagga edition), and I have not seen it treated as it deserves by other writers. I make no reference to developments of Buddhist Philosophy in the N. and E. of Asia. I speak only of the relatively narrow world in which the good and learned Buddhaghosācariya moved and thought and wrote—a striking embodiment of the meticulous erudition, the piety, the complacent sectarian view, the amazing credulity, the absence of curiosity as to the greater world so characteristic of his epoch. And I anticipate that our knowledge of his little world, and his interpretation of its 'Buddhism' will be placed on a better basis by Mr. Law's book.

C. A. F. RHYS DAVIDS.

CHIPSTEAD, SURREY:
October 26th, 1921.

PREFACE

BUDDHAGHOSA was the most celebrated commentator of the Theravāda School of Buddhism. An attempt has been made in the present treatise to build up a connected history of the life and labours of the distinguished exegete. In the first chapter, I have attempted to put together the materials for a life-history of Buddhaghosa as culled from his own works as well as from Dhammakitti's account recorded in the Mahāvaṁsa. The second chapter deals with the legends which grew about our commentator as mentioned in the Buddhaghosuppatti, the Sāsanavaṁsa and similar works. Much importance cannot be attached to these legends as they are of little value from the historical point of view. The third chapter treats of the origin and development of Buddhist commentaries, and an important branch of the Buddhist literature, namely, that of the Porāṇas has been examined in it. I am indeed thankful to Mrs. Rhys Davids for kindly drawing my attention to this point. In the fourth chapter dealing with the works of Buddhaghosa, I have discussed about the ascription of the authorship of the Dhammapada commentary to our commentator. A Sanskrit poem, Padyacūḍāmaṇi, attributed to Buddhaghosa and lately published by the Government of Madras, has also been noticed in it. I have omitted the Jātaka commentary from my list of the works of Buddhaghosa although this may appear to be somewhat astounding to many. A careful comparison of the style and language of the Jātaka commentary with the style and language of the works of Buddhaghosa shows convincingly that the Jātaka commentary was not the composition of Buddhaghosa. I agree with T. W. Rhys Davids when he says that the date of this Jātaka commentary is unknown. I am not prepared to accept the native tradition in Ceylon that the original Jātaka book was written in Sinhalese and was translated into Pāli by Buddhaghosa; and the Sinhalese original was afterwards lost as Cowell says in his preface to the first volume of the Jātaka. In the opening verses of the Jātaka commentary, the name of the author is not mentioned. Childers goes so far as to identify the author of the Jātaka commentary with Buddhaghosa. I have great doubt as to the correctness of the theory that Buddhaghosa was the author of the Jātaka commentary. But there is no satisfactory evidence to set the controversy at rest one way or the other. Chapter V treats of the successors of Buddhaghosa. An account has been given in the following chapter of the versatile intellect of Buddhaghosa and the encyclopædic character of his works. In this chapter I have also devoted a few pages to an account of Buddhaghosa's knowledge of anatomy. The commentator never fails to say a few words about the subject whenever he has the chance. In the Visuddhimagga, in the commentaries on the Khuddaka-Pāṭha and the Vibhaṅga, he makes repeated references to matters of anatomical interest. He is rather learned for his day in anatomy and takes care that his readers should know it, as Mrs. Rhys Davids points out. Chapters VII and VIII deal with his philosophy and interpretation of Buddhism. Many knotty points of Buddhist philosophy and many important terms of Buddhist doctrine received lucid treatment at his hands. Many other important points connected with the history of Buddhaghosa, as for example, the commentator's knowledge as to the details of Vedic sacrifices, have also been treated in the following pages.

It is not an easy task to construct a connected biography of Buddhaghosa, as most of his works are buried in manuscripts. Some of his works have been printed in Ceylonese and Burmese characters. The Pāli Text Society of England have published some in Roman character. I have tried to utilize almost all his works as well as the documents that furnish any information regarding him.

The present treatise is, I believe, the first of its kind and about four years ago, at the request of my teacher, the late Mahāmahopādhyāya Dr. Satish Chunder Vidyābhūṣaṇa, M.A., Ph.D., I wrote a prolegomenon to it under the name, "A Note on Buddhaghosa's commentaries" which was published in the Journal of the Asiatic Society of Bengal.

I am indebted to Mrs. Rhys Davids, D.Litt., M.A., who has been kind enough to help me with many valuable suggestions and to write a foreword to the present work. I am also indebted to Mr. Haran Chunder Chakladar, M.A., and Dr. Hem Chunder Rai Chowdhury, M.A., Ph.D., P.R.S. for their suggestions. I am thankful to Dr. Narendranath Law for including this humble treatise in his Calcutta Oriental Series.

My thanks are due to the Offg. Director-General of Archæology, India; Superintendent, Archæological Survey, Central Circle, Patna; Mr. Ramaprasad Chanda, B.A.,

F.A.S.B., Superintendent, Archæological Section, Indian Museum, Calcutta; and Messrs. W. E. Bastian & Co., Colombo, Ceylon, for the photographs and for their kind permission to reproduce them in this book.

BIMALA CHARAN LAW.

24, SUKEA'S STREET,
CALCUTTA,
April, 1923.

CONTENTS

ILLUSTRATIONS

THE
LIFE AND WORK OF BUDDHAGHOSA

CHAPTER I

THE LIFE OF BUDDHAGHOSA

Pre-eminence of Buddhaghosa.

In the history of Pāli Buddhist literature, the name of Buddhaghosa stands out pre-eminent as that of the greatest commentator and exegctist. Buddhaghosa did for the Pāli Tripiṭaka what Sāyaṇa did for Vedic literature. Many a word and expression, many points of Buddhist theology and many cruces of philosophy would not have been clearly intelligibe to later generations but for the immense labour that Buddhaghosa bestowed upon the exegesis of the Pāli texts. Besides mere verbal glosses and philological discussions, Buddhaghosa has introduced in his commentaries an immense mass of legends and fables, folk-tales and traditions, history and biography, which has made his works a huge store-house from which the historian of ancient Indian sociology can draw without end. Our great regret, however, is that very little is known about the personal history of this great expounder of the Buddha's words. Buddhaghosa was one of those many Indian celebrities who have left for us no other records of their career than their teachings and works to be appraised for what they are worth. This is, however, precisely the fate which the great sons of India

Paucity of biographies in Ancient India.

themselves sincerely desired. It is comforting to think that what they have concealed from us is but the details of their daily life, their worries and anxieties, and what they have given us is the most valuable record of their inner life and experience. And yet while reading through their works, we feel a burning desire to know something about the persons themselves, to live over again with them the life they actually lived, the things they actually saw, and, above all, to prepare ourselves by their examples to fight the great battle of life and to confront once more the deeper problems of humanity. These are the feelings that come irresistibly ; but the materials to build up a biography are scanty

Materials for the life-history of Buddhaghosa.

So far as Buddhaghosa is concerned, we have nothing except his commentaries and a few traditions and legends. To make a close and careful study of his commentaries and to separate the few grains of biographical detail from the mass of extraneous matter is a Herculean task ; the traditions preserved are so meagre and so much coloured by the after-thoughts of the later ages of credulity that it seems at first sight to be an impossible task to obtain any reliable information from them. And yet in the last resort these late traditions and myths are the only materials on which an authentic account of his life-history has to be based. Besides the meagre references that Buddhaghosa himself has made to the details of his life in his great commentaries, the earliest connected account that has come down to us of his life-history, is that contained in the second part of chapter XXXVII of the great Ceylonese chronicle, the Mahāvaṁsa.

This section, however, is considered to be later than the remaining portions of the chronicle, having been added by Dhammakitti, a Ceylonese Sramaṇa of the middle of the 13th century. This compilation of the great commentator's life-history, though made after the lapse of more than eight hundred years since the time when he lived, is not altogether unworthy of credence and is very probably derived from older materials; our only regret is that it tells us so little. We make, therefore, no apology for giving here the whole of the brief account furnished by Dhammakitti.

Dhammakitti's account of Buddhaghosa.

The Mahavaṁsa, while giving an account of the reign of king Mahānāma who ruled in Ceylon in the early years of the fifth century A.C., narrates the following story about the life and labours of Buddhaghosa.[1] "A Brāhman youth,

[1] Mahāvaṁsa (Turnour), pp. 250–253. Cf Andersen's Pāli Reader, pp. 113-114.
"Bodhimaṇḍasamīpamhi jāto brāhmaṇamānavo,
Vijjāsippakalāvedī tīsu vedesu pārago,
Sammāviññātasamayo sabbavādavisārado,
Vādatthī Jambudīpamhi āhiṇḍanto pavādino
Vihāraṁ ekaṁ āgamma rattiṁ Pātañjali-mataṁ
parivatteti saṁpuṇṇapadaṁ suparīmaṇḍalaṁ.
Tatth'eko Revato nāma mahāthero vijāniya,
'Mahāpañño ayaṁ satto, dametuṁ vaṭṭatīti' so
'Ko nu gadrabharāvena viravanto'ti abruvi,
'gadrabhanaṁ rave atthaṁ kiṁjānāsīti' āha taṁ.
'Ahaṁ jāne' ti vutto so otāresi sakaṁ mataṁ,
Vuttaṁ vuttaṁ viyākāsi virodhaṁ pi ca dassayi,
'Tena hi tvaṁ sakaṁ vādaṁ otārehi,' ca codito
pāliṁ āhābhidhammassa, atthaṁ assa na so'dhigā.
Āha: 'kass'eso manto' ti, 'Buddhamanto' ti so'bruvi,
'dehi me tan' ti vutte hi 'gaṇha pabbajja taṁ' iti.
Mantatthī pabbajitvā so uggaṇhi Piṭakattayaṁ,

born in the neighbourhood of the terrace of the great Bo-tree (in Magadha), accomplished in the 'vijjā' and 'sippa,' who

'ekāyano ayaṁ maggo' iti pacchā taṁ aggahi.
Buddhassa viya gambhīraghosattā naṁ viyākaruṁ
'Buddhaghosa ti, so sobhi' Buddho viya mahītale.
Tattha Ñānodayaṁ nāma katvā pakaranaṁ tadā
Dhammasaṅgaṇiyākāsi kaṇḍaṁ so Atthasāliniṁ.
Parittaṭṭhakathañ c'eva kātuṁ ārabhi buddhimā,
taṁ disvā Revato thero idaṁ vacanaṁ abruvi:
'Pālimattaṁidhānītaṁ, n'atthi Aṭṭhakathā idha,
tathācariyavādā ca bhinnarūpā na vijjare,
Sīhalaṭṭhakathā suddhā Mahindena matīmatā
Saṅgītittayaṁ ārūḷhaṁ Sammāsambuddhadesitaṁ
Sāriputtādigītañ ca kathāmaggaṁ samekkhiya
katā Sīhalabhāsāya Sīhalesu pavattati.
Taṁ tattha gantvā sutvā tvaṁ Māgadhānaṁ niruttiyā
parivattehi, sā hoti sabbalokahitāvahā.'
Evaṁ vutto pasanno so nikkhamitvā tato imaṁ
dīpaṁ āgā imass'eva rañño kāle mahāmati.
Mahāvihāraṁ sampatto vihāraṁ sabbasādhunaṁ
Mahāpadhānagharaṁ gantvā Saṁghapālassa santikā
Sīhalaṭṭhakatham sutvā theravādañ ca 'sabbaso
Dhammassāmissa eso va adhippāyo' ti nicchiya
Tattha saṁghaṁ samānetvā 'kātuṁ aṭṭhakathaṁ mama
potthake detha sabbe' ti āha. Vimaṁsituṁ sa taṁ
Saṁgho gāthādvayaṁ tassa dāsi: 'sāmatthiyaṁ tava
ettha dassehi, taṁ disvā sabbe demāti potthake.'
Piṭakattayaṁ etth'eva saddhiṁ Aṭṭhakathāya so
Visuddhimaggaṁ nāmākā saṁgahetvā samāsato.
Tato saṁghaṁ samūhetvā Sambuddhamatakovidaṁ
Mahābodhisamīpaṁhi so taṁ vācetuṁ ārabhi.
Devatā tassa nepuññaṁ pakāsetuṁ mahājane
chādesuṁ potthakaṁ, so pi dvattikkhattuṁ pi taṁ akā.
Vācetuṁ tatiyevāre potthake samudāhaṭe
potthakadvayaṁ aññaṁ pi saṇṭhapesuṁ tahiṁ marū.
Vācayiṁsu tadā bhikkhū potthakattayaṁ ekato,
ganthato atthato vāpi pubbāparavasena vā
Theravādehi pālihi pādehi vyañjanehi ca

had achieved the knowledge of the three "Vedas," and possessed great aptitude in attaining acquirements, indefatigable as a schismatic disputant, and himself a schismatic wanderer over Jambudīpa, established himself in the character of a disputant in a certain vihāra, and was in the habit of rehearsing, by night and by day with clasped hands, a discourse which he had learnt, perfect in all its component parts, and sustained throughout in the same lofty strain. A certain mahāthera, Revata, becoming acquainted with him there and (saying to himself), 'This individual is a person of profound knowledge; it will be worthy (of me) to convert him'; enquired, 'who is this who is braying like an ass?' (The Brāhmaṇa) replied to him, 'Thou canst define, then, the meaning conveyed in the bray of asses.' On (the thera) rejoining, 'I can define it'; he (the Brāhmaṇa) exhibited the extent of the knowledge he possessed. (The thera) criticised each of his propositions and pointed out in what respect they were fallacious. He who had been thus refuted, said, 'well, then, descend to thy own creed'; and he propounded to him a passage from the "Abhidhammo" (of the Piṭakattaya).

---

aññathattaṁ ahu n'eva potthakesu pi tīsu pi.
Atha ugghosayi saṁgho tuṭṭhahaṭṭho visesato:
'Nissaṁsayaṁ sa Metteyyo' iti vatvā punappunaṁ
Saddhiṁ Aṭṭhakathāyādā potthake Piṭakattaye,
Ganthākare vasanto so vihāre dūrasaṁkare
Parivattesi sabbā pi Sīhalaṭṭhakathā tadā
sabbesaṁ mūlabhāsāya Māgadhāya niruttiyā.
Sattānaṁ sabbabhāsānaṁ sā ahosi hitāvahā,
theriyācariyā sabbe Pāliṁ viya taṁ aggahuṁ.
Atha kattabbakiccesu gatesu pariniṭṭhitiṁ
Vandituṁ so Mahābodhiṁ Jambudīpaṁ upāgami."

He (the Brāhmaṇa) could not divine the signification of that (passage); and enquired, 'whose manto is this?' 'It is the Buddha's manto.' On his exclaiming, 'Impart it to me'; (the thera) replied, 'Enter the sacerdotal order.' He who was desirous of acquiring the knowledge of the Piṭakattaya, subsequently coming to this conviction: 'This is the sole road (to salvation)' became a convert to that faith. As he was as profound in his (ghoso) eloquence as the Buddha himself, they conferred on him the appellation of Buddhaghoso (the voice of the Buddha); and throughout the world he became as renowned as the Buddha. Having there (in Jambudīpa) composed an original work called 'Ñānodayam' he, at the same time, wrote the chapter called 'Atthasālinī on the Dhammasaṅgaṇi (one of the commentaries on the Abhidhammo). Revata thera then observing that he was desirous of undertaking the compilation of a "Paritta-aṭṭhakatham" (a general commentary on the Piṭakattaya), thus addressed him: 'The text alone (of the Piṭakattaya) has been preserved in this land: the Aṭṭhakathā are not extant here; nor is there any version to be found of the vādā (schisms) complete. The Sinhalese Aṭṭhakathā are genuine. They were composed in the Sinhalese language by the inspired and profoundly wise Mahindo, who had previously consulted the discourses of the Buddha, authenticated at the three convocations, and the dissertations and arguments of Sāriputto and others, and they are extant among the Sinhalese. Repairing thither, and studying the same, translate (them) according to the rules of the grammar of the Māgadhas. It will be an act conducive to the welfare of the whole world.' Having been thus advised, this eminently wise personage rejoicing therein, departed from thence, and visited this island in the reign of this monarch (Mahānāma). On reaching the Mahāvihāra (at Anurādhapura) he entered the Mahāpadhāna Hall, the most splendid of the apartments in the vihāra, and listened to the Sinhalese Aṭṭhakathā, and the Theravādā, from the beginning to the end, propounded by the thera Sanghapāli; and became thoroughly convinced that they conveyed the true meaning of the doctrines of the Lord of Dhammo. Thereupon paying reverential respect to the priesthood, he thus petitioned: 'I am desirous of translating the Aṭṭhakathā; give me access to all your books.' The priesthood for the purpose of testing his qualifications gave only two gāthās saying: 'Hence prove thy qualification; having satisfied ourselves on this point, we will then let thee have all our books.' From these (taking these gāthās for his text), and consulting the Piṭakattaya, together with the Aṭṭhakathā and condensing them into an abridged form, he composed the commentary called the 'Visuddhimaggam. Thereupon having assembled the priesthood who had acquired a thorough knowledge of the doctrines of the Buddha, at the Bo-tree, he commenced to read out (the work he had composed). The devatās in order that they might make his (Buddhaghosa's) gifts of wisdom celebrated among men, rendered that book invisible. He, however, for a second and third time, recomposed it. When he was in the act of producing his book for the third time, for the purpose of propounding it, the devatās restored the other two copies also. The (assembled) priests then read out the three books simultaneously. In those three versions, neither in a signification, nor in a single misplacement by transposition; nay even in the thera controversies, and in the text (of the Piṭakattaya), was there in the measure of a verse, or in the letter of a word, the slightest variation. Thereupon the priesthood rejoicing, again and again fervently shouted forth, saying, 'Most assuredly this is Metteyyo (Buddho) himself'; and made over to him the books in which the Piṭakattaya were recorded, together with the Aṭṭhakathā. Taking up his residence in the secluded Ganthākāro vihāro at Anurādhapura, he translated, according to the grammatical rules of the Māgadhas, which is the root of all languages, the whole of the Sinhalese Aṭṭhakathā (into Pāli). This proved an achievement of the utmost consequence to all languages spoken by the human race. All the Theras and Ācariyas held this compilation in the same estimation as the text (of the Piṭakattaya). Thereafter, the objects of his mission having been fulfilled, he returned to Jambudīpa to worship at the Bo-tree (at Uruvelāya in Magadha)."

Credibility of the account of Dhammakitti.

The thirty-three couplets quoted in the foot-note are, as we have said before, from the supplementary chapter of the Mahāvaṁsa written by Dhammakitti in the 13th century A.C. It was written several centuries after Buddhaghosa lived and compiled his works, but Dhammakitti must have had some authentic records before him from which he drew his information. He might have got the account, as the late Prof. Rhys Davids says,[1] from "the tradition as preser-

[1] Hastings, Encyclopædia of Religion and Ethics, Vol. II., p. 886.

ved at the Great Minster in Anurādhapura in written documents now no longer extant." The whole account here given in the Mahāvaṁsa has the impress of truth on it with the exception, of course, of the portion speaking of the share the Devas took in augmenting the glory of Buddhaghosa.

Credibility of the date of Buddhaghosa as given by Dhammakitti.

The most important service that Dhammakitti renders to our knowledge of the great sage, is that he fixes definitely the time when Buddhaghosa lived. The king Mahānāma reigned in the first half of the fifth century A.C., as the Ceyionese chronicle shows; and as Buddhaghosa visited Ceylon and worked there during this period, we can be certain about the age he lived in. In the great darkness that hangs over the history of Indian literature, whether Sanskrit or Pāli and in view of the uncertainty which perplexes us whenever we make an attempt to fix the date of any great Indian author with anything like definiteness, the value of this simple fact that we know of Buddhaghosa's time is inestimable.

The date given by Dhammakitti is also substantiated by internal evidence derived from the commentaries of Buddhaghosa himself. Buddhaghosa shows his acquaintance with the Milinda Pañho. This is clear from two passages pointed out by Rhys Davids, one from Buddhaghosa's commentary on the Mahāparinibbāṇa Sutta (vi. 3) and the other from his comment on the Ambaṭṭha Sutta (Dīgha Nikāya, III. 2, 12) where the great exegete refers to and quotes from the conversation between Milinda and Nāgasena. Dr. Morris has pointed out two other passages making similar quotations from the Milinda Pañho, one of them from the Manorathapūraṇī, Buddhaghosa's commentary on the Aṅguttara Nikāya, and the second from his commentary on the Majjhima Nikāya, the Papañcasūdanī.[1] These passages as given in Buddhaghosa's works, do not agree very closely, word for word, with the text of the Milinda Pañho as edited by Mr. Trenckner, but the substance is the same, so that there cannot be any reasonable doubt that Buddhaghosa did actually know the Milinda Pañho. In view of the respect with which he speaks about it, there can be no question, as Rhys Davids points out, that the Questions of King Milinda "must have been written some considerable time before Buddhaghosa."[2] Mrs. C. A. F. Rhys Davids draws our attention to several passages in the Atthasālinī, that is, Buddhaghosa's commentary on the Dhammasaṅgaṇi,[3] where he refers to Āyasmā Nāgasena, Nāgasenatthera, Āyasmā Nāgasenatthera, Thera Nāgasena, or simply the Thera. In her edition of the Visuddhimagga of Buddhaghosa, the learned author has discovered at least three passages which can be traced to the Milinda Pañho.[4] References to other post-canonical Buddhist works, such as the Peṭakopadesa, Anāgatavaṁsa besides some of the ancient aṭṭhakathās and other works which are no longer extant, have been pointed out by the same gifted lady in the works of Buddhaghosa already referred to.

[1] For these quotations, see Rhys Davids, The Questions of King Milinda, S.B.E., xxxv., pp. xiv–xviii.

[2] Ibid., p. xxv.

[3] Mrs. Rhys Davids, A Buddhist Manual of Psychological Ethics, p. xxiv

[4] Visuddhimagga (P.T.S.), Vol. II., p. 761.

But it is to be observed that in none of these cases, there is the least reason for thinking that any of the works quoted from or referred to by Buddhaghosa, was of a later date than what is alloted to him by Dhammakitti. There can, therefore, be no hesitation in accepting the first half of the fifth century A.C. as the time when Buddhaghosa lived and wrote his works.

The Burmese tradition as recorded by Bishop Bigandet also points to the beginning of the fifth century A.C. as the time when the great commentator visited the shores of the Martaban. Thus writes the Bishop in his 'Life or Legend of Gaudama' "It is perhaps as well to mention here an epoch which has been at all times famous in the history of Buddhism in Burma. I allude to the voyage which a Religious[2] of Thaton, named Budhagosa, made to Ceylon, in the year of religion 943-400 A.C. The object of this voyage was to procure a copy of the scriptures. He succeeded in his undertaking. He made use of the Burmese or rather Talaing characters, in transcribing the manuscripts, which were written with the characters of Magatha. The Burmans lay much stress upon that voyage, and always carefully note down the year it took place. In fact, it is to Budhagosa that the people living on the shores of the Gulf of Martaban owe the possession of the Buddhist scriptures. From Thaton, the collection made by Budhagosa was transferred to Pagan, six hundred and fifty years after it had been imported from Ceylon."

---

1 Buddhaghosa's Parables by Capt. T. Rogers, p. xvi., f. n. i.

2 A 'religious' is 'one bound by monastic vows.'

Buddhaghosa's proficiency in Brahmanical learning.

It will be apparent from the previous discussion that the date of Buddhaghosa as given by Dhammakitti accords with all known facts. Dhammakitti's account of Buddhaghosa's proficiency in the Vedas and in other branches of Brahmanical learning is also substantially correct. It is confirmed by internal evidence from the great exegete's own commentaries. Buddhaghosa in his Sumaṅgalavilāsinī makes mention of the four vedas, viz. Irubbeda (Rigveda) Yajubbeda (Yajurveda) Sāmaveda and Athabbaṇa Veda.[1] He also shows his acquaintance with the details of Vedic sacrifices. He says that yiṭṭha is called the great sacrifice (mahāyāga) and huta is hospitality offered to the persons attending the sacrifice. He speaks of aggihoma[2] which, he adds, derives its name from the fact that it is performed by burning sacrificial things in fire produced by wood. According to him, dabbihoma is a kind of aggihoma and is so called because this sacrifice is performed by putting husks into the fire by means of a wooden spoon. He says that kaṇo is red powder which adheres to the grain of rice under the husk. Taṇḍula includes sāli-rice and other grasses. Sappi is go-sappi, (cow-ghee), etc. Tela is sesamum oil, etc. The sacrifices called mukha homa and lohita homa have also been referred to by our author in his Sumaṅgalavilāsinī. The former is spoken of as a kind of sacrifice in which the mustard seeds, etc., are thrown in the fire by taking them in the mouth and the latter is a kind of sacrifice

---

1 Sumaṅgala-Vilāsinī (P.T.S.), pt. I., p.247.

2 Sumaṅgala-Vilāsinī (P.T.S.), pt. I., p.93.

performed by the blood of the right knee, etc.[1] According to Buddhaghosa, saddha is a food prepared for the dead, thālipāka is a food prepared for a good ceremony such as marriage, etc. yañña is a food prepared for a sacrifice and pāhuna is a food prepared for the guests, it also means food for presentation.[2] We are also told that those who perform the great sacrifice (mahāyāgaṁ) by raising big sacrificial posts, writing on them the names of such and such a king or the names of such and such a brahmin, do not cut trees or dubba grasses, not to speak of the killing of the cows, goats and the like.[3] Buddhaghosa does not keep us in the dark as to what he thought regarding the brahmanical practices. He says that the brahmins though versed in the three Vedas, have not seen Brahmā.[4] They offer prayers for help to Inda, Soma, Varuṇa, Isāna, Pajāpatī, Brahmā, Mahiddhi and Yama. But the commentator does not find any good result following from such prayers.[5]

It must not be thought that the Vedic texts were the only brahmanical works known to Buddhaghosa. He gives us a derivation of the word, 'Itihāsa,'[6] which agrees almost exactly with the explanation given by Yāska in his Nirukta. He shows his knowledge of the place where the Brāhmaṇas used to stay from time to time to repeat their mantras.[7] In

---

1 Sumaṅgala-Vilāsinī, p.93. 2 Sumaṅgala-Vilāsinī, pt. I., p.267. 3 Ibid., p.300.

4 Sumaṅgala-Vilāsinī, (U. Phye's edition), p.292. 5 Ibid, p.292.

6 Sumaṅgala-Vilāsinī, p. 247.

"Athabbaṇa-Vedaṁ catutthaṁ katvā itiha āsa itiha āsāti īdisa-vacana paṭisaṁyutto purāṇa-kathā-saṁkhāto itihāso pañcamo."

7 Dialogues of the Buddha, pt. I., p. 300.

his Visuddhimagga[1] dealing with the virtue of Titikkhā, i.e. forbearance, he says, "A person endowed with the quality of forbearance is one whom I call Brāhmaṇa." In his Parables, he refers to brahmanical rites.[2] He refers the expression, Bandhupādāpaccā, to the brahman theory that Sudras were born from Brahmā's heels.[3] That he was acquainted with the history of the Brahmin religious sects is apparent from the account he gives of the eight different sorts of Brāhmaṇ ascetics discussed in the Journal of the Pāli Text Society, 1891, and from the commentary of the Saṁyutta Nikāya where we find that he went so far as to investigate the history of Dhanañjanī brahmins who according to him, "were one of the most aristocratic families claiming to have sprung not from the mouth but from the splitting open of the head of Brahmā." His comments upon the Pāli passage[4] relating to the supplementary treatise of the Vedas cannot be expected from one who was not conversant with the whole of the Vedic literature. His emphasis on Vinaya is another proof of the influence of his previous learning. His definitions of killing, theft, etc., indicate an enormous improvement on older expositions. He had knowledge of some of the systems of Hindu philosophy. His knowledge of Sāṅkhya philosophy is shown by his attitude towards pakativāda as it will be seen in a subsequent chapter. He enriched his Buddhist heritage with fresh materials from other systems; consider, for example, his use of the term 'Samūha' which reminds us at once of

---

[1] P.T.S. Edition, p. 295. [2] Buddhaghosa's Parables, p. lxxvii f.n.

[3] Dialogues of the Buddha, pt. I., p. 112.

[4] Sumaṅgala-Vilāsinī, pt. I., p. 247.

Patañjali's Mahābhāṣya.[1] There are many other similar passages.[2]

Agreement of Dhammakitti's account of the life of Buddhaghosa with the evidence of the commentaries.

Now we shall proceed to show that the account given by Dhammakitti of the life of Buddhaghosa agrees generally with what the great exegetist has said about himself in his own commentaries, specially in the Nidānakathā or story of the origin of the works at their respective beginnings. Thus in the Nidānādikathā to his Visuddhimagga, Buddhaghosa at the very beginning quotes the following gāthā of Buddha's own saying:—

"Sīle patiṭṭhāya naro sapañño, cittaṁ paññaṁ ca bhāvayam,
Ātāpī nipako Bhikkhu, so imam vijaṭaye jaṭanti."

(After having been established in precepts, a wise person should think of samādhi and paññā, an active and wise Bhikkhu disentangles this lock.) Next he proceeds to record the circumstances under which he wrote this great compend-

---

1 See Patañjala-darṣanaṁ by Jīvānanda Vidyāsāgara, p. 375, cf. the passage quoted in Vyāsa's Commentary on Yoga Sūtra, III., 44.

"Sāmānya viśeṣa samudāyotra dravyaṁ,
dviṣṭho hi samūhaḥ pratyastamita bhedāvayavānugataḥ
sarīraṁ vrikṣo yuthaṁ vanaṁiti.........."
"Ayutasiddha vayavabhedānugataḥ samūho
dravyamīti Patañjaliḥ" (Ibid., p. 376). Cf. Atthasālinī,
p. 61. "Samūhasaṅkhāto pana samayo anekesaṁ
sahuppattiṁ dīpeti." Çf. Sangahasaddo, p. I.
Cf. Ibid., p. 167. "paṭhavī kāyo paṭhavī samuha va."

2 Paramatthajotikā on the Sutta-Nipāta. II., Vol. I., p. 169. "Athavā sante na kurute iti sante na sevatīti attho, yathā rājānaṁ sevatīti etasmiṁ atthe rājānaṁ pakurute ti saddavidū mantenti." It is an application of the rule of Pāṇini, 1–3–32. "Gandhanāvakshepaṇa sevana sāhasikya pratiyatna prakathanopayogeṣu kriñaḥ."

ium of Buddhism : 'The real meaning of sīla, etc., is described by means of this stanza uttered by the great sage. Having acquired ordination in the Order of the Jina (conqueror) and the benefit of the sīla, etc., which is tranquil and which is the straight path to purity, the Yogis who are desirous of obtaining purity, not knowing purity as it is, do not get purity though they exert. I shall speak of the Visuddhimagga according to the instruction of the dwellers of the Mahāvihāra, which is pleasing to them and which is the correct interpretation : Let all the holymen who are desirous of obtaining purity listen to what I say, attentively.[1]

At the end of the work again, Buddhaghosa returns to that very gāthā which he has adopted as his text for writing the Visuddhimagga, and after referring to his promise quoted above, thus delivers himself :

'The interpretation of the meanings of the sīla, etc., has been told in the Aṭṭhakathās on the five Nikāyas. All of them being taken into consideration, the interpretation gradually becomes manifest, being free from all faults due to confusion ; and it is for this reason that the Visuddhimagga

---

1 Visuddhimagga (P.T.S.), Vol. I., p. 2.

"Imissā dāni gāthāya kathitāya mahesinā
vaṇṇayanto yathābhūtaṁ atthaṁ sīlādibhedanaṁ,
sudullabhaṁ labhitvāna pabbajjaṁ Jinasāsane,
sīlādisangahaṁ khemaṁ ujuṁ maggaṁ visuddhiyā,
yathābhūtaṁ ajānantā, suddhikāmā pi ye idha
visuddhiṁ nādhigacchanti vāyamantā pi yogino,
tesaṁ pāmojjakaranaṁ suvisuddhavinicchayaṁ
Mahā-vihāravāsīnaṁ desanānayanissitaṁ
Visuddhimaggaṁ bhāsissaṁ ; taṁ me sakkaccabhāsato
visuddhikāmā sabbe pi nisāmayatha sādhavo ti."

should be liked by the Yogis who are desirous of obtaining purity and who have pure wisdom.'

Taking the consent of the revered Sanghapāla who is wise, who is pure and devoted to sīlas, who observes the rules of Vinaya and who is devoted to the Order and whose mind is full of the qualities of forbearance, delight and love, etc., and who belongs to the family of the dwellers of the Mahāvihāra who are the famous theras and who are the foremost amongst the Vibhajjavādins, this has been composed by me for the long existence of the True Law. On account of the power of the merit acquired by me without any hindrance, let all creatures obtain happiness. The Visuddhimagga has been finished in 58 chapters without any obstacle. Let all the good desires of the world be fulfilled quickly, without any hindrance.[1]

Here we observe that according to Buddhaghosa, the

---

[1] Visuddhimagga, Vol. II., pp. 711 and 712.

" Tesaṁ sīlādibhedānaṁ atthānaṁ yo vinicchayo,
pañcannaṁ pi Nikāyānaṁ vutto Aṭṭhakathānaye:
Samāharitvā taṁ sabbaṁ yebhuyyena vinicchayo,
sabbasankaradosehi mutto yasmā pakāsito,
Tasmā visuddhikāmehi suddhapaññehi yogihi
Visuddhimagge etasmiṁ karaṇīyo va ādaro ti.
Vibhajjavādi-seṭṭhānaṁ theriyānaṁ yasassinaṁ,
Mahāvihāravāsīnaṁ vaṁsajassa vibhāvino:
Bhadantasanghapālassa sucisallekhavuttino,
Vinayācārayuttassa yuttassa paṭipattiyaṁ.
Khantīsoraccamettādi-guṇabhūsitacetaso,
ajjhesanaṁ gahetvā va karontena imaṁ mayā;
Saddhammaṭṭhitikāmena yo patto paññasañcayo;
tassa tejena sabbe pi sukhamedhentu pāṇino
Visuddhi-Maggo eso va antarāyaṁ vinā idha,
niṭṭhito aṭṭhapaññāsa bhāṇavarāya Pāḷiyā

whole of this great work of his was written as a commentary on that one gāthā uttered by the Master. Evidently it was this gāthā which Dhammakitti had in his mind when he wrote that the Visuddhimagga was written as a comment on and expansion of the two gāthās which were set by the Sinhalese Saṅgha residing at the Mahāvihāra to test Buddhaghosa's learning and efficiency.

Dhammakitti also records that the wonder-struck theras of the Mahāvihāra likened the author of the Visuddhi-Magga to Maitreya and it will be observed that Buddhaghosa also reminds himself of the same Bodhisatta when he finally lays down his pen as shown by the two final verses[1] the translation of which is as follows:—

At the last birth as a human being, seeing Metteyya who is the great sage, who is the foremost of all men, who is the lord and who is devoted to the welfare of all beings and listening to the preaching of the true law of the wise, I may shine in the Order of the Jina, having obtained the best fruit.

In the Nidānakathā to his Atthasālinī or commentary on the Dhammasaṅgaṇi, Buddhaghosa also speaks of the circumstances under which his commentary was compiled from the Sinhalese Aṭṭhakathās composed by Mahinda and preserved in Ceylon and herein he also refers to the work done

---

Yathā tath'eva lokassa sabbe kalyāṇanissitā,
Anantarāyā ijjhantu sīghaṁ sīghaṁ manorathāti."

[1] Visuddhimagga (P.T.S.), Vol. II., p. 713.
"Antime attabhāvamhi Metteyyaṁ munipungavaṁ,
lokaggapuggalaṁ nāthaṁ sabbasattahite rataṁ
Disvāna tassa dhīrassa sutvā saddhammadesanaṁ
adhigantvā phalaṁ aggaṁ sobheyyaṁ Jinasāsanaṁ ti."

by him in his Visuddhimagga. Thus he goes on: "I will set forth, rejoicing in what I reveal, the explanation of the meaning of that Abhidhamma as it was chanted forth by Mahā Kassapa and the rest (at the first council), and re-chanted later (at the second council) by the Arahats, and by Mahinda brought to this wondrous isle and turned into the language of the dwellers therein. Rejecting now the tongue of the men of Tambapaṇṇi and turning it into that pure tongue which harmonizes with the texts (I will set it forth) showing the opinion of the dwellers in the Great Minster, undefiled by and unmixed with the views of the sects and adducing also what ought to be adduced from the Nikāyas and the commentaries."[1] Explaining the decision of the Bhikkhus of the Mahāvihāra, which is unmixed with the opinions of the followers of other Nikāyas, I shall explain the meaning, word for word, of all texts (tanti), taking what is to be taken from āgamaṭṭhakathās and satisfying the learned ones but excluding all the kammaṭṭhānas, cariya (conduct) abhiññā (supernatural knowledge) vipassanā (insight) as they have been explained in the Visuddhimagga.[2]

---

1 Mrs. C. A. F. Rhys Davids, A Buddhist Manual of Psychological Ethics, pp. xxii-xxiii. Atthasālinī (P.T.S.), pp. 1–2., Verses 13-19.
"Yā Mahākassapādīhi vasīh' aṭṭhakatha purā
saṅgītā anusaṅgītā pacchā pi ca isīhi yā
Ābhatā pana therena Mahindena taṁ uttamaṁ
yā dīpaṁ dīpavāsīnaṁ bhāsāya abhisaṅkhatā.
Apanetvā tato bhāsaṁ Tambapaṇṇinivāsinaṁ
āropayitvā niddosaṁ bhāsaṁ tantinayānugaṁ
Nikāyantaraladdhīhi asammissaṁ anākulaṁ."

2 "Mahāvihāravāsīnaṁ dīpayanto vinicchayaṁ
Atthaṁ pakāsayissāmi āgamaṭṭhakathāsu pi

In the introductory verses to his Sumaṅgalavilāsinī or commentary on the Dīgha-Nikāya also, Buddhaghosa makes similar references to the history of the composition of his commentaries. Thus he observes: "Through the influence of serene mind and merit which are due to the salutation of the Three Refuges and which put an end to obstacles, in order to explain the meaning of the Dīgha-Nikāya containing long suttas, which is a good āgama, described by the Buddhas and minor Buddhas and which brings faith, the Aṭṭhakathās have been sung and afterwards resung from the beginning by 500 theras, and are brought to the island of Laṅkā by the wise Mahinda and put in the language of the island of Laṅkā for the welfare of its inhabitants. Discarding the Sinhalese language and rendering them into a good language which is like Tanti and which is free from faults and not rejecting the explanations of the theras who are the dwellers of the Mahāvihāra, who are the lamps of the group of theras and who are good interpreters, I shall explain the meaning, avoiding repetitions, for the delight of the goodmen and for the long existence of the dhamma."[1]

---

gahetabbaṁ gahetvāna tosayanto vicikkhaṇe.
Kammaṭṭhānāni sabbāni cariyābhiññā vipassanā
Visuddhimagge pan' idaṁ yasmā sabbaṁ pakāsitam
Tasmā taṁ agahetvāna sakalāya pi tantiyā
padānukkamato eva karissām' atthavaṇṇanaṁ."
Sumaṅgalavilāsinī, pt. I., p. I.

[1] "Iti me pasannamatino ratanattayavandanāmayaṁ puññaṁ
Yaṁ suvihatantarāyo hutvā tassānubhāvena
Dīghassa dīghasuttaṁkitassa nipuṇassa āgamavarassa
Buddhānubuddhasaṁvaṇṇitassa saddhāvahaguṇassa,
Atthappakāsanatthaṁ aṭṭhakathā ādito vasisatehi

Here also he refers to his Visuddhimagga[1]: "I shall not again discuss what has been well told in the Visuddhimagga. Standing in the midst of four āgamas, the Visuddhimagga will explain the meaning which has been told there, this being done, you will understand the meaning of the Dīgha Nikāya taking it along with this Aṭṭhakathā (i. e. Sumaṅgalavilāsinī)."

In the Sumaṅgalavilāsinī, he also refers to his Samantapāsādikā, Vinayaṭṭhakathā (Sumaṅgalavilāsinī, I, p. 70). In this last work, Buddhaghosa mentions by name some of the Sinhalese commentaries,[2] such as the Mahā-Aṭṭhakathā or the great commentary or the commentary of the Mahāvihāra at Anurādhapura, the Mahāpaccarī or the Great Raft Commentary which, Buddhaghosa says in his Papañcasūdanī, was so named from the fact of its having been composed on a raft

Pañcahi yā saṁgītā anusaṁgītā ca pacchā pi
Sīhaḷadīpaṁ pana ābhatātha vasinā Mahā-Mahindena
Ṭhapitā Sīhaḷabhāsāya dīpavāsinaṁ atthāya.
Apanetvāna tato' haṁ Sīhaḷabhāsaṁ manoramaṁ bhāsaṁ
Tantinayānucchavikaṁ āropento vigatadosaṁ
Samayaṁ avilomento therānaṃ theravaṁsappadīpānaṁ
Sunipuṇavinicchayānaṁ Mahāvihārādhivāsīnaṁ
Hitvā punappunāgataṁ atthaṁ atthaṁ pakāsayissāmi
Sujanassa ca tuṭṭhatthaṁ ciraṭṭhitatthañ ca dhammassa."
Sumaṅgalavilāsinī, pt. I., p. 2.

[1] "Itipana sabbaṁ yasmā Visuddhimagge mayā suparisuddhaṁ
Vuttaṁ tasmā bhīyo na taṁ idha vicārayissāmi.
Majjhe Visuddhimaggo esa catunnaṁ pi āgamānaṁ hi
Ṭhatvā pakāsayissati tattha yathā bhāsitaṁ atthaṁ
Icceva kato tasmā taṁ pi gahetvana saddhiṁ etāya
Aṭṭhakathāya vijānātha dīghāgamanissitaṁ atthaṁ ti."

[2] Vide "Origin of the Buddhist Aṭṭhakathās," J.R.A.S. 1871, p. 295.

in Ceylon and the Kuruṇḍa Aṭṭhakatha, that is, the commentary written at Kurundavelu Vihāra, in Ceylon. These commentaries besides other post-canonical books have been quoted from or referred to by Buddhaghosa in his works; those mentioned in the Atthasālinī have been pointed out by Mrs. Rhys Davids.[1]

In the epilogue to his commentary on the Vinaya Piṭaka, Buddhaghosa tells us that he completed his great work in the twenty-first year of the reign of king Sirinivāsa of Ceylon, who was his benevolent royal patron[2]. Perhaps he refers to the same king under the name of Sirikūṭa in the epilogue to his commentary on the Dhammapada.[3] It is left to further research to settle whether or not Sirinivāsa was another name of King Mahānāma, during whose reign our Commentator visited Ceylon according to the Mahāvaṁsa. The Rev. Bhikkhu H. P. Buddhadatta is of this opinion. He points out that nowhere else is mentioned a King of Ceylon by the name of Sirikūṭa or Sirinivāsa.

Buddhaghosa refers to King Duṭṭhagāmaṇī Abhaya,[4] the national hero of Ceylon, and to King Coranāga,[5] son of king Vaṭṭagāmaṇī. He also makes mention of a king named Mahānāga whose magnificent gifts in connection with the art of healing at Penaṁbarigana won for him a lasting fame.[6] King Mahānāga is perhaps no other than King Buddhadāsa,

---

[1] A Buddhist Manual of Psychological Ethics, pp. XXIII—XXIV.

[2] "Palāyantassa sakalam Laṅkādīpaṁ nirabbudaṁ rañño Sirinivāsassa samavisatime kheme jayasamvacchare ayaṁ. Āraddha ekavisaṁhi sampatte pariniṭṭhitā ti."

[3] Dhammapada-Aṭṭhakathā, P.T.S., Vol. IV, p. 235.

[4] Atthasālinī, p. 81. [5] Ibid, p. 399. [6] Ibid, p. 399.

father of King Mahānāma mentioned in the Mahāvaṁsa (Chap. XXX. 171.) Buddhaghosa refers to Cetiyapabbata of Ceylon where a king went out by the eastern gate to reach the pabbata and reached the banks of the Colombo river, the horse standing on the bank was not willing to get down into the river like the horse Guḷavaṇṇa of King Kūṭakaṇṇo.[1]

As we have seen from the quotations made from the introductory verses of his commentaries, Buddhaghosa says that Mahinda brought the Aṭṭhakathā (rehearsed by five hundred Bhikkhus at the first council) to Ceylon,[2] and in the Sumaṅgalavilāsinī, he speaks of Mahinda as the person who not only brought the Aṭṭhakathā into Ceylon but also rendered it into Sinhalese for the good of the inhabitants of the island.[3] This confirms the tradition of the Mahāvaṁsa which attributed the authorship of the whole of the Sinhalese Aṭṭhakathā to Mahinda.

Buddhaghosa in his Sāratthapakāsinī refers to Thera Mahāmahinda who, when he came to the island, sat at Jotivana and preached the doctrine and, it is added, the earth quaked.[4]

He also refers to various Vihāras of Ceylon which may be enumerated thus:—

1. Colombotittha Vihāra[5] where fifty Sinhalese monks used to take their abode in the rainy season.

---

1 Sāratthapakāsinī (mss) p. 25. "Kūṭakaṇṇarañño Guḷavaṇṇasso viya, Rājā kira pacinadvārena nikkhamitvā 'Cetiyapabbataṁ gamissāmīti' kalambanadītīraṁ sampatto asso tīre ṭhatvā udakam otaritum na icchati"

2 Sāratthapakāsinī, (mss) p. 1.

3 Sumaṅgalavilāsinī, p. 1. 4 p. 29.

5 Sāratthapakasinī (mss) p. 132.

2. Girikaṇḍaka Vihāra in the village of Vattakālaka in Ceylon, where a householder's daughter on account of her strong faith in the Buddha got Ubbegapīti and soared into the sky.[1]

3. Mahāvihāra[2] where there were resident Bhikkhus whose teaching was in the language of the text (tanti).

4. Mahāvihāra[3] where the excellent Aṭṭhakathā or commentary was written.

A reference is also made to Tipiṭaka Cūḷābhaya of Mahāvihāra who mastered the Aṭṭhakathā.[4] A thera of Ceylon named Cittagutta who was an inhabitant of Kuraṇḍaka Mahāleṇa, is referred to in the Visuddhimagga.[5] Koraṇḍaka was a vihāra in Ceylon where a thera used to live as mentioned in the Visuddhimagga.[6] A reference is made to a thera named Mahāddhammarakkhita who used to live in a vihāra of Ceylon named Tulādharapabbata.[7]

We have tried to put together here what we know of the history of Buddhaghosa. This, as we have said, is too meagre to satisfy our cravings for information about the life of the great commentator, whose industry has rendered the Pāli Buddhist literature and philosophy intelligible to us.

---

1 Atthasālinī, p. 116.

2 Ibid, p. 2.

3 Sāratthapakāsinī (mss) p. 2. verse 10. "Sunipuṇa Vinicchayānaṁ Mahāvihārārādhivāsīnaṁ hitvā punappunāgatamatthaṁ atthaṁ pakāsayissāmi sujanassa ca tuṭṭhatthaṁ ciraṭṭhitathañca dhammassa."

4 Visuddhimagga, Vol. I, p. 96.

5 Ibid, p. 38. 6 Ibid, p. 91. 7 Ibid. p. 96.

CHAPTER II

LEGENDS ABOUT BUDDHAGHOSA

Legendary accounts of Buddhaghosa.

We have seen in the last chapter that the account of Buddhaghosa as given in the supplement to the Mahāvaṁsa is in the main worthy of credence. In course of time, however, a mass of legends grew about the few simple facts noted by Dhammakitti. Such legends are found in the Buddhaghosuppatti, also known as the Mahābuddhaghosassa Nidānavatthu, by the priest Mahāmaṅgala about whose life and date we know hardly anything. He was most probably a Ceylonese by birth as pointed out by Gray,[1] and evidently lived after the time when the Mahāvaṁsa account was written. Besides the Buddhaghosuppatti, other late works of the southern Buddhist school, such as the Gandhavaṁsa,[2] the Sāsanavaṁsa,[3] and the Saddhamma Sangaha,[4] furnish some additional details. But the accounts of all these works are of the nature of legends in which fact and fiction are often hopelessly blended together. The authors have given free scope to their imagination and introduced poetical and rhetorical embellishments, rendering it difficult to dissociate the grains of authentic biography from the chaff of fable and fiction that has accumulated round the name of the great scholar. J

1 Buddhaghosuppatti, p.33.

2 J. P. T. S.. 1886, p.66.

3 P. T. S., 1897, edited by Miss Bode.

4 J. P. T. S, 1890, p.55.

Gray has brought together the accounts of the life of Buddhaghosa from these and other sources, Talaing, Sinhalese, and Burmese. We give below a summary of the story of Buddhaghosa derived mainly from the materials collected by Gray, providing additional information from works like the Gandhavaṁsa and the Saddhammasangaha.

Birth of Buddhaghosa in a brahmin family.

After the death of Thera Mahinda there appeared, in course of time, a thera named Buddhaghosa.[1] There was a village named Ghosa not far from the great Bo-tree; this village was called Gosagāma, as it was inhabited by a large number of cowherds. A certain king[2] ruled at that time and he had a brahmin chaplain (purohita) named Kesī who was the foremost among the preceptors of his time. Kesī had a wife named Kesiṇī.[3] At that time it was found very difficult to understand the teachings of the Lord as they were written in Sinhalese. A certain thera who possessed supernatural powers and was free from sins, thought thus: "Who is that

[1] According to the Burmese tradition, Buddhaghosa was born in Northern India in the fifth century A.D. in the country of Magadha. (cf. Buddhism as a religion by Hackmann, p. 68).

[2] King Saṅgrāma who ruled in Magadha at the beginning of the fifth century A.D. Kesī was his spiritual adviser. (Jagajjyotiḥ, Āṣāṛ 1315, B.S. Pt. II).

[3] It is recorded in the Sāsanavaṁsa that Buddhaghosa was a native of Ghosagāma near the Bodhi terrace. The brahmin Keśa was his father and Kesī his mother (p. 29).

"Mahātherā....Ghosaṁ.....yācitvā bodhirukkhasamīpe Ghosagāme Keṣassa nāma brāhmaṇassa Kesiyā nāma brāhmaṇiyā kucchimhi paṭisandhiṁ gaṇhāpesum." The Sāsanavamsa (p. 30) further narrates that Thera Buddhaghosa was born in a brahmin village near the great Bo-tree. ("Buddhaghosathero nama mahābodhirukkhasamīpe ekasmiṁ brāhmaṇagāme vijāto.")

great thera who will be able to render the teachings of the Lord into the Māgadhi language from the language of Ceylon?" Thinking thus he saw clairvoyantly that there lived a celestial being in the Tāvatiṁsa heaven, who would be competent to perform the task. Thereupon the thera appeared before Sakka who asked him as to the cause of his coming. He informed Sakka about his mission. Sakka asked him to wait a little. The chief of the Tāvatiṁsa devas then approached a deva named Ghosa and enquired, "Do you wish to go to the human world?" The deva replied, "I desire to go to a still higher celestial world and not to the human world where there is much suffering: but if the teaching of the Lord is difficult for the human beings to understand, I am ready to go there." Thus he consented and his consent was made known to the thera who was a friend of the brahmin Kesī. The thera next went and told Kesī, "During seven days from this day, don't plunge into worldly enjoyments; a son will be born to you who will be very wise and virtuous." Saying this the thera left him. Exactly on the seventh day, the deva Ghosa, after death, was reborn in the womb of Kesiṇī. After ten months he was born, and to him as a babe, slaves, hired servants, and brahmins uttered sweet words, 'eat, drink.' The boy is said to have been named Ghosa on account of these utterances.[1]

His education.

When Ghosa was seven years old, he learnt the Vedas and within seven

[1] Buddhaghosuppatti p. 39, cf. Sāsanavaṁsa, p. 29.
"Khādatha bhonto pivatha bhonto ti ādi brāhmaṇānaṁ aññamaññaṁ ghosakāle vijāyanattā Ghosoti nāmaṁ akāsi."

years, he acquired mastery over the three Vedas. One day he was eating peas sitting on the shoulder of Viṣṇu. Seeing him thus seated, the other brahmins grew angry and said, "Why are you eating peas sitting on the shoulder of our teacher Viṣṇu; you do not know your own measure, how will you know the three Vedas?" Ghosa replied, "The Māsa (pea) itself is Viṣṇu; what is it that is called Viṣṇu?—of these two, how can I know which is Viṣṇu?" The brahmins could not give any reply, they merely looked at one another. They were struck dumb, and informed Kesī all about it. Kesī asked his son, "Have you behaved like this?" Ghosa replied in the affirmative. Thereupon Kesī consoled the brahmins thus, "Don't be angry, he is young." The brahmins went away thus consoled.[2]

Kesī used to instruct the king in the Vedas. One day he went to the king, accompanied by his son. While instructing his royal pupil, he came on a passage in which some knotty points were involved. He could not make out their meaning, and with the king's permission, returned home. Ghosa being aware of it, secretly wrote the meaning of those difficult points in the book for the benefit of his father. The brahmin Kesī became highly satisfied when he saw the purport and meaning of the points which had puzzled him, written down in the book, and enquired who had actually done it. He was informed by the members of his family that his son was the writer. Thereupon the

---

1 Cf. Sāsanavaṁsa, p. 29.
"Sattavassikakāle so tiṇṇaṁ vedānaṁ pāragū ahosi."

2 Buddhaghosuppatti, (Edited by J. Gray) pp. 37–40.

brahmin asked his son, "Dear, is this writing yours?" The boy replied in the affirmative. Kesī lost no time in informing the king of it. The latter greatly delighted, embraced the young Ghosa, kissed his forehead, saying, "You are my son, I am your father," and rewarded him with an excellent village.[1]

His conversion.

Ghosa learnt the Vedas and he got by heart six thousand padas daily. One day a great thera who was a friend of Kesī, went to the latter's house to take his food. Ghosa's seat was allotted to him and the thera being indifferent as to whose seat it was, sat on it. Ghosa became angry. seeing the great thera seated on his seat, and he abused the latter thus, "This shaven-headed Samana is shameless; he does not know his measure. Why has my father invited him? He does not know the Vedas or another cult." He resolved to ask him questions regarding the Veda as soon as he finished his meal. Accordingly he asked the thera, "Do you know the Veda or any other cult?" Mahāthera being greatly pleased said, "Oh, Ghosa, I know your Vedas or any other cult." Ghosa said, "If you know the Vedas, please recite." Then the Mahāthera recited the three Vedas, fully bringing out the significance of the knotty points. Ghosa was charmed by his recitation and said thus, "I want to know your cult, please recite. The Mahāthera then recited the contents of the Abhidhamma with special reference to kusala dhamma, akusala dhamma and abyākata dhamma. He also explained some difficult problems of

[1] Buddhaghosuppatti, (Ed. by J. Gray) pp. 40–41.

Buddhist philosophy which were afterwards incorporated in the Atthasālinī, a commentary on the Dhammasaṅgaṇi. Altogether twenty-one kinds of kusala dhamma, twelve kinds of akusala dhamma, thirty-six kinds of vipāka (consequence) and twenty kinds of kiriyācitta were mentioned by the Mahāthera. While listening to the exposition of saddhamma (true law), Ghosa was utterly charmed and said, "What is your cult? Can a householder learn it?" He was told that it could be learnt by a monk. Ghosa said, "The cult of the Buddha is invaluable, it pleases me; when one has learnt it, he becomes free from all suffering." He then informed his parents that he intended to renounce the world. He said, "I shall take ordination from the Mahāthera, learn the cult of the Buddha and then I shall come back home being disrobed." His parents consented after some hesitation and took him to the Mahāthera and spoke to him thus, "This is your grandson, who is desirous of receiving ordination from you, give him ordination." Ghosa was ordained and was given Tacakammaṭṭhāna.[1] On asking the meaning of Tacakammaṭṭhāna, he received the following reply, "Meditate upon kesa, loma, nakha, danta, and taco." All Buddhas realised the fruition of saintship depending on Tacakammaṭṭhāna.[2] Ghosa listened to it, meditated thereon and became established in the Three Refuges. He practised the ten precepts, having acquired a firm faith in the

---

[1] Buddhaghosuppatti, pp. 42-45.

[2] Kammaṭṭhāna means analytical meditation or contemplation. Buddhaghosa in his Visuddhimagga has enumerated forty Kammaṭṭhānas. Tacakammaṭṭhāna means meditation on hair, nails, teeth, and skin.

teaching of the Lord. He told the thera, "Sir, the teaching of the Lord puts an end to suffering; my Vedas are worthless and they are rightly given up by the Buddha and other saints."[1] Thus he obtained ordination from the hands of the Mahāthera. The name of the Buddhist Elder is not mentioned in the second chapter of the Buddhaghosuppatti where the details of Ghosa's conversion have been noted. According to the Saddhamma Sangaha,[2] it was one Revata who gave him ordination after he had embraced Buddhism. It is stated there that a young brahmin wandered through villages, countries, towns, and capital cities of Jambudvīpa and defeated everybody, by answering questions put to him. At last he came to a monastery; there many hundreds of the Order dwelt; of these the Thera Revata was the foremost, who was free from sin, who had acquired analytical knowledge and who used to defeat other disputants. The young brahmin was one day chanting the mantras and the thera listened to the recitation and said, "Who is this braying like an ass?" The youth replied, "Oh, monk! how will you know the meaning involved in the braying of an ass?" The thera said, "Yes, I know." He was thereupon asked

[1] Buddhaghosuppatti, Tr. p. 11.

[2] pp. 51–52 (J. P. T. S. 1890) "Bho brāhmaṇa, ahaṁ tayā bahu-pucchito, ahaṁ pdāni taṁ ekaṁ pañhaṁ pucchāmi, vyākarissasi me pañhaṁ ti. Āma bho pabbajita puccha vyākarissāmīti. Thero cittayamake imam pañham pucchi: Yassa cittaṁ uppajjati, na nirujjhati tassa cittaṁ nirujjhissati nuppajjissati, yassa vā pana cittaṁ nirujjhissati, nuppajjhissati tassa cittaṁ upajjissati na nirujjhissatīti. Brāhmaṇo uddhaṁ vā adho vā harituṁ asakkonto: Kinnāma bho pabbajjita idan ti āha. Buddha-manto nāmāyaṁ brāhmaṇāti. Sakkā pana tam bho mayhaṁ pi dātum ti. Sakkā brāhmaṇa amhehi gahita-pabbajjaṁ gaṇhantassa dātum ti. Tato brāhmaṇo mantatthāya pabbajjaṁ yāci. Thero brāhmaṇaṁ pabbājetvā upasaṁpādes."

questions regarding all knotty points involved in the three Vedas, the Itihāsas, etc. The thera answered them correctly. At last the thera said to his young interlocutor, "Oh, Brāhmin, you have asked me many questions, I ask you only one, please answer it." The young man replied, "Ask me any question, I am ready to answer." The thera put a question to him from the Cittayamaka in the book of the Yamaka. The brahmin was unable to answer it, and asked for ordination from him for the sake of the mantra. The thera ordained him and accepted him as a novice. A similar account is recorded in the Mahāvaṁsa as we have seen in the previous chapter.

The Ceylonese mission contemplated.

Here is another interesting incident of his life. One day Ghosa who was in a solitary place, thought, "Is my knowledge greater or that of my preceptor, so far as the teaching of the Lord is concerned." The preceptor, by thought-reading, knew of the question that had arisen in the mind of Ghosa and he said to him thus, "If you think thus, it is unworthy of you."[1] Ghosa begged his pardon and repented saying, "It is my sin, pardon me." The preceptor replied, "I will pardon you if you go to Ceylon and render the teaching of the Lord into the Māgadhi language from the language of Ceylon."[2] Ghosa said, "If you desire it, I also

---

[1] Cf. Sāsanavaṁsa, p. 29. "Buddhabhāsite piṭakattaye mama vā paññā adhikā udāhu upajjhāyassa vā ti."

[2] Cf. Sāsanavaṁsa, p. 29. "......tvaṁ āvuso Sīhaladīpaṁ gantvā piṭakattayaṁ Sīhalabhāsakkharena likhitaṁ Māgadhabhāsakkharena likhāhi evaṁ sati ahaṁ khamissāmīti āha."

desire to go to the island of Ceylon, yet let me stay here till I remove the false belief of my father."

The story about the conversion of Buddhaghosa's father.

When Ghosa returned to his father Kesī, the latter thought thus, "My son will now be a householder." Breaking his silence, he asked Ghosa whether he would be a householder now. Ghosa did not reply.[1] He was maturing plans for persuading his father to give up his false belief and become a follower of the Buddha.

It is interesting to mention here how Ghosa is represented as succeeding in this task. He went to his own dwelling-place and caused two inner rooms to be built, making a roof of brick and plastering it with mud and covering it with planks. In one of the two rooms, he fitted up two bolts both inside and outside; there he kept fire, pot, rice, water, milk, curd, ghee, etc. And shutting the door of the room by a mechanism, he caused his father to enter the room. Kesī said, "Dear, I am your father, why are you behaving like this?" Ghosa replied, "It is true that you are my father, but as you are a heretic and have no faith in the teaching of the Lord, I have inflicted such punishment upon you." The father replied, "I do not cherish false belief, open the door." Ghosa said, "If you do not, then speak of the virtues of the Lord in the words, "Iti pi so Bhagavā, etc." (the orthodox formula of the faithful) He filled his father's mind with pious fear, saying, "If you do not give up false belief, you will fall into hell after death."

---

[1] Buddhaghosuppatti, p. 46.

Kesī spent three days there and on the fourth day, he recollected the virtues of the Lord told by his son and uttered the words, "Iti pi so Bhagavā, etc.," and acquired a spotless faith in the Three Refuges. He admitted that the Buddha was his Satthā (teacher). He was established in the fruition of the First Path. Ghosa now opened the door of the room, bathed his father with scented water and asked his pardon. Kesī praised the Lord in verses. Ghosa became greatly delighted in listening to the words of his father. Thus Kesī gave up the false belief which he cherished so long, through the exertions of his son.[1]

Visit to Ceylon.

After having established his father in the fruition of the first stage of sanctification, Ghosa begged his pardon and returned to his preceptor. No sooner did he get permission from his preceptor to go to Ceylon than he directed his steps towards the shore together with some merchants and boarded a ship which sailed at once. On his way to Ceylon,[2] he met a thera named Buddhadatta who was then coming back to Jambudvīpa from Laṅkā.[3] Buddhaghosa safely reached Laṅkādvīpa. There he went to the Saṃgharāja Mahāthera, saluted him and sat on one side just behind the monks who were learning Abhidhamma and Vinaya.[4] One day the

---

1 Buddhaghosuppatti edited by J. Gray, pp. 47–48. Cf. Sāsanavaṁsa edited by M. Bode, p. 29. "Buddhaghoso ca pitaraṁ micchādiṭṭhibhāvato mocetvā...."

2 On his way to Ceylon, before he met Buddhadatta, he reached Nāgapaṭṭana. Saddhamma-Saṅgaho, J.P.T.S., 1890, p. 53. "....Nāgapaṭṭanaṁ sampāpuni."

3 Buddhaghosupp[illegible]ti, p. 49.

4 It is recorded in [illegible]e Sāsanavaṁsa (Edited by Mabel Bode, p. 31) that Buddhaghosa went to Ceylo[illegible] [illegible]ad he entered the Mahāvihāra at Anurādhapura. There

chief of the congregation, while instructing the monks, came upon a knotty point, the meaning and purport of which he could not make clear. He was struck dumb and went to his inner chamber and sat there thinking upon it. Ghosa knew all about it and wrote out on a black board the purport and meaning of the knotty point and when the chief of the congregation came out of his inner chamber, he looked at the writing. The Saṁgharājā enquired, "Who has written this?" He was told by the hermits thus, "It must have been written by the stranger monk." The chief enquired, "Where has he gone?" The hermits sought him out and showed him to the chief. The chief enquired whether it was written by him and getting a reply in the affirmative, said, "The congregation of monks should be taught by you in the three Piṭakas." Ghosa refused, saying, "I have come here to translate the teachings of the Lord from Sinhalese into Māgadhi." On hearing this, the chief became pleased and said, "If you have come here to perform such a task, you make clear to us the significance of the following stanza uttered by the Buddha in reference to the three Piṭakas:—

Buddhaghosa's learning tested.

Who is that person who being wise and established in the precepts, and having cultured his thoughts and wisdom, being ardent and skilful, can unravel this knot?" Ghosa

---

having listened to the Sinhalese Aṭṭhakathā and Theravāda from Thera Saṁghapāla he said that he would prepare an aṭṭhakathā himself.

"Buddhaghosathero Sīhaladīpaṁ gantvā Anurādhapure Mahāvihāraṁ pavisitvā Saṁghapālatherassa santike saddhiṁ Sīhalaṭṭhakathāya theravāde sutvā aṭṭhakathaṁ karissāmīti ārocesi.

consented, saying, "All right," and returned to his abode. On the very day in the afternoon, he wrote out the Visuddhimagga very easily, beginning with sīle patiṭṭhāya, etc. After writing the Visuddhimagga, he fell asleep. Sakka, the chief of the gods, stole it. On awaking, he could not find out his own composition and wrote out the Visuddhimagga again, as quickly as possible, by lamplight. After completing it, he kept it on his head and again fell asleep. Sakka stole it for the second time. The thera awaking could not find it, he again wrote it as quickly as possible. After completing it, he fell asleep by tying it to the garment he wore. Sakka then left the two books already stolen by him, on his head.[1] In the morning Ghosa was delighted to see his books on his head. After ablution, he showed the three books to the chief of the congregation of the monks at Laṅkā.[2] It is interesting to note that in these three books, there were more than one million nine hundred and twenty-three thousand letters, particles and prefixes. The chief became astounded and asked him as to the reason of his writing out the same book three times. Ghosa told him the reason. Then the three books were recited.[3] It is to be noticed that the particles, prefixes and letters were the same and were put in the same places in all the three books.[4] The chief noticing this feature, became greatly pleased and gave the author permis-

[1] Cf. Saddhamma-Saṁgaho, J.P.T.S. 1890, p. 53. ".... devatā dve potthake tassa adāsi."

[2] Cf. Sāsanavaṁsa, p. 30.

[3] Cf. Saddhamma-Saṅgaho, J.P.T.S., 1890, p. 53 "...... bhikkhu-saṁgho tīṇi-potthakāni ekato vācesi."

[4] Cf. Saddhamma-Saṅgaho, J.P.T.S., 1890, pp. 53–54 "Ganthato vā akkharato vā

sion to render the teaching of the Lord into Māgadhi from Sinhalese. The chief spoke highly of the merits of Ghosa. Since then he became famous as Buddhaghosa among the inhabitants of Ceylon.[1] He was called the chief of the human beings like the Buddha on earth.[2]

Buddhaghosa engaged in translating scriptures.

While in Ceylon, Buddhaghosa used to live on the lower flat of a seven-storied building. There he was engaged in translating the teachings of the Lord daily;[3] in the morning when he used to go out for alms, he would see palm-leaves which had fallen and taking them he would depart from the place to which he had come to beg. This was his practice while he was at Ceylon. One day a toddy-seller who was wise and experienced, saw his acts, scattered on the place of his begging unbroken palm-leaves and then hid himself. The thera when he had finished begging, carried them to his house. The toddy-seller followed him, saw him actually engaged in writing and was satisfied. One day he took a potful of food and presented it to the thera. The thera said to him, "There lives a superior thera on the upper flat, please give it to him." The toddy-seller went upstairs and when he met the thera on the upper flat, the latter said, " Buddhaghosa who

---

padato vā vyañjanato vā atthato vā pubbāparavasena vā theravādādīhi vā pāḷihi vā tīsu potthakesu aññathattaṁ nāma nāhosi."

1 Cf. Saddhamma-Saṃgaho, J.P.T.S. 1890, pp. 52–53 " Tatopaṭṭhāya so bhikkhu Buddhaghosatthero nāmāti loke pākaṭo ahosi."

2 Buddhaghosuppatti, p. 58.

3 According to Spence Hardy, Buddhaghosa took up his residence in the secluded Ganthākāra Vihāra where he was occupied with the work of translating, according to the grammatical rule of the Māgadhi which is the root of all languages, the whole of the Sinhalese Aṭṭhakathās into Pāli. (A Manual of Buddhism, p. 531).

dwells on the lower flat is worthier than we, daily he translates the teachings of the Lord into Māgadhi, give it to him." The toddy-seller, thereupon, returned to Buddhaghosa and offered the food to him. He accepted it and made six shares out of it and gave one share to each of the six theras.

Buddhaghosa's task of translating was finished in three months. Having observed the Pavāraṇā, he informed the chief of the congregation of the completion of his task. The Samgharājā praised him much and set fire to all the works written by Mahinda in Sinhalese; Buddhaghosa now asked the permission of the congregation to go home and see his parents. While he was going to embark, the Sinhalese monks spoke ill of him thus, "We are of opinion that this thera knows the Tripiṭakas, but he does not know Sanskrit." As soon as Buddhaghosa heard this, he at once addressed the chief of the congregation of Sinhalese monks thus, "Revered Sir, to-morrow, on the Sabbath-day, I shall give an address in Sanskrit; let the four-fold assembly gather together in the yard of the great shrine." Early in the morning, he in the midst of the congregation ascended the pulpit to display his knowledge of Sanskrit and uttered some stanzas in Sanskrit, the purport of which is as follows[1] :—

Buddhaghosa's knowledge of Sanskrit displayed.

"Subsisting as a porter, a cowherd, a water-drawer, or by serving the learned, is excellent. I beg you to let me hold up my hands in adoration; let not the three worlds by the seven offences disgustingly besmear the conchshell-like

[1] Buddhaghosuppatti, p. 61.

religion of the adorable one, the son of Suddhodana—a religion worthy to be reverenced by the head; besmear yourselves with virtue that is like sandal-wood; otherwise destroying yourselves, death is preferable."[1]

Then he got down from his pulpit and saluted the congregation of monks. Since then the monks had no doubt as to his knowledge of Sanskrit.

The quick wisdom of Buddhaghosa.

The following event which is said to have happened while Buddhaghosa was in Ceylon, is worthy of notice. One day two maid-servants of two brahmins fell out with each other. When one of them was walking up the bank of a pond taking a jar of water, the other was coming down in a hurry with one empty jar which collided with that of the former. The maid-servant whose jar was broken, was angry and abused the other who also abused her. Buddhaghosa hearing this, thought thus, "There is nobody here, these women abusing each other would surely speak to their masters about it and I might be cited as a witness." The master of the maid-servant whose jar was broken, referred the matter to the tribunal; the king not being able to decide the case asked, "Who is your witness?" One of the maids referred to Buddhaghosa who was introduced to the king as a stranger, who received the punishment of the Church. Appearing before the king, Buddhaghosa observed, "The abusive language used by the maid-servants of the brahmins has been heard by me. We, monks, take no notice of such things." Saying this, he hand-

1. Buddhaghosuppatti, translation, p. 30.

ed over a book in which he had recorded the abusive language. His Majesty decided the case relying on the written evidence of Buddhaghosa. The brahmins spoke ill of Buddhaghosa saying, "This discarded monk has come to trade, you should not see him." The king, however, praised the latter by saying that he (Buddhaghosa) was a man of quick wisdom and enquired as to where he lived. He said, "I have never seen before a Samaṇa like him who is religious, of quick intellect and greatly meditative."[1]

Return of Buddhaghosa to India.

On returning from Ceylon, our monk, first of all, went to his preceptor in the Jambudvīpa and informed him that he had written the Pariyatti. Paying his respect to his spiritual guide, he went home to his parents who gave him excellent food to take.[2]

Story of Buddhaghosa's visit to Burma.

Some are of opinion that after having completed his work in Ceylon, Buddhaghosa came to Burma to propagate the Buddhist faith.[3] The Burmese ascribe the new era in their religion to the time when the great exegete reached their country from Ceylon.[4] He is said to have brought over from that island to Burma, a copy of Kaccāyana's Pāli Grammar which he translated into Burmese. He is credited with having written a commentary upon it. It is not, however, mentioned by the great Pāli grammarian and lexicographer,

[1] Buddhaghosuppatti, pp. 53-54.
[2] do. p. 63.
[3] Manual of Indian Buddhism by Kern, p. 125.
[4] Manual of Buddhism by Spence Hardy, p. 532.

Moggallāna (A.D. 1153–1186), nor by the Prākrit grammarians Hem Chandra and others and must apparently be placed amongst the supposititious works of Buddhaghosa.[1] A volume of Parables in Burmese language is also attributed to him.[2] The Burmese Code of Manu, too, is said to have been introduced into Burma from Ceylon by the same Buddhist scholar.[3] But the code itself is silent on this point. Professor Hackmann says, "There is ground for doubting the statement that this man brought Buddhism to Burma. The chronicles of Ceylon to which we owe the information about Buddhaghosa, and which must have been well-informed on the subject, give no account of his journey to further India. Indeed one of the most important inscriptions in Burma, which was erected at the end of the fifth century A.D., at the instance of a King of Pegu, who was among the most devoted adherents of Buddhism, and which throws a backward glance over the history of Buddhism in Burma, makes no mention whatsoever of Buddhaghosa. The Burmese tradition which refers to him does so on account of his translations and writings having become fundamental in the country, probably also because his intellectual influence may have inaugurated a new epoch in Burmese Buddhism."[4]

We are of opinion that although the chronicles of Ceylon and the inscriptions of the fifth century A.D. erected at Burma, are silent on this point, yet his works, e.g. the Atthasālinī, the Visuddhimagga, etc., were well-known to the Bur-

---

1 Indian Antiquary, Vol. XIX, 1890 (April), p. 119.

2 Ibid, p. 119.　3 Ibid, p. 119.

4 Buddhism as a religion by H. Hackmann, p. 68.

mans and held in high esteem by them from a very early time. Even now Buddhaghosa is so much adored and worshipped by the Burmans that he appears actually to have lived amongst them.

Death of Buddhaghosa.

We are to record here the death of the great commentator as described in the Buddhaghosuppatti.[1] The exact time of his own death was known to him and he thought thus, "Death is of three kinds, samuccheda, khaṇika and sammuti. Of these, samuccheda is the death of one without taint, khaṇika is the momentary cessation of thought production, sammuti is the ordinary death of all living beings and of these am I to die the common death?" Even at the last moment of his life, he was in the habit of philosophising. Bearing in mind the precepts to be observed, he expired and was reborn in the Tuṣita heaven. We do not know where he breathed his last.[2] His commentaries are silent on this point.

His funeral.

After his death, a funeral bed of sandal wood was prepared by all gods and men, Samaṇas and Brāhmaṇas, on which to burn his dead body. After his dead body had been cremated, Brahmins and other persons took the relics, buried them in sacred spots near the Bodhi tree and erected stūpas over them.[3]

A word or two is necessary here about the historical

---

[1] pp. 65-66.

[2] The inhabitants of Cambodia are of opinion that Buddhaghosa died in their country in a great monastery named Buddhaghosa-Vihāra which is very old.

[3] Buddhaghosuppatti, p. 66.

value of the Buddhaghosuppatti or the history of the rise and career of Buddhaghosa. A critical examination of the work does not assist us much in elucidating the history of Buddhaghosa The author had little authentic knowledge of the great commentator. He only collected the legends which centred round the remarkable man by the time when his work was written. Those legends are mostly valueless from the strict historical point of view. Gray truly says in his introduction to the Buddhaghosuppatti that the work reads like an "Arthurian Romance." As we shall show presently, the accounts given by the Buddhaghosuppatti about the birth, early life, conversion, etc., of Buddhaghosa, bear a striking similarity with those of Milinda and Moggaliputta Tissa. In the interview which took place between Buddhaghosa and Buddhadatta, the latter is said to have told Buddhaghosa thus, "I went before you to Ceylon to compile Buddha's word, I am old, have not long to live and shall not, therefore, be able to accomplish my purpose. You carry out the work satisfactorily." In the Vinayavinicchaya which is attributed to Buddhadatta, we find that during the meeting, Buddhadatta requested Buddhaghosa to send him the commentaries when finished, that he might summarise them. Accordingly Buddhaghosa sent him the commentaries and Buddhadatta summarised the commentary on the Abhidhamma in the Abhidhammāvatāra and the commentary on the Vinaya in the Vinayavinicchaya. The above statement in the Vinayavinicchaya which is more authoritative than the Buddhaghosuppatti, is in direct contradiction

Historical value of the Buddhaghosuppatti.

to the statement in the latter work. In the sixth chapter of the Buddhaghosuppatti, it is stated that Buddhaghosa rendered the Buddhist scriptures into Māgadhi and in the seventh chapter, it is stated that when after three months, he completed his task, the works of Mahendra (Mahinda) were piled up to a height seven times that of a middle-sized elephant in a holy spot near the great shrine and burnt. It is evident that the author in the sixth chapter has made a mistake. Buddhaghosa translated the Sinhalese commentaries into Māgadhi and not the texts themselves. Had it been so, there would not have been any occasion for setting fire to the works of Mahendra. On the other hand, they would have been carefully preserved as the only reliable and authentic interpretation of the sacred texts. It has been distinctly stated in the Mahāvaṁsa that the texts only existed in the Jambudvīpa and Buddhaghosa was sent to Ceylon to translate the Sinhalese commentaries into Māgadhi. If the tradition recorded in the Mahāvaṁsa is to be believed, then only we can get an explanation for the destruction of Mahinda's works.

Possible sources of Buddhaghosa legends.

It is interesting to note that the incidents connected with the birth, early life, and conversion of Buddhaghosa fully resemble those connected with the birth, early life, and conversion of Nāgasena as recorded in *The Questions of King Milinda*. Before his birth, Nāgasena was a deva living in a happy world and consented to come down to earth only at the request of the Arahats to uphold the teachings of the Buddha. Buddha

Story of Nāgasena.

ghosa, according to the Buddhaghosuppatti, was also a deva living in the next world, and came down to earth at the request of Sakka to translate the Sinhalese scriptures into Pāli. Both Buddhaghosa and Nāgasena are said to have showed wonderful signs of intelligence in their boyhood. Both mastered the Vedas within a very short time. Both were converted at a very early age by theras who used to visit their houses. The incidents in the lives of both these celebrities after conversion, are similar. After ordination Nāgasena thought one day that his teacher must be a fool, in as much as he instructed him first in the Abhidhamma to the exclusion of other teachings of the Buddha. His teacher who was an Arahat, immediately came to know what was passing in the mind of Nāgasena and rebuked him for entertaining such thoughts. Nāgasena apologised, but his teacher said, "I will not forgive you until you go and defeat King Milinda who troubles the monks by asking questions from the heretic's point of view." According to the Buddhaghosuppatti, Buddhaghosa, too, one day reflected, "Am I or my preceptor more advanced in the Buddha's words." His teacher knowing his mind, said, "Buddhaghosa, your thoughts please me not; if you reflect thus, you will see that they are not becoming of a priest; beg my pardon." Thereupon Buddhaghosa apologised, but his teacher said, "I shall pardon you if you go to Ceylon and render the Buddha's scriptures into Pāli."

Story of Moggaliputta Tissa.

The story of the conversion of Buddhaghosa also tallies with that of Moggaliputta Tissa as recorded in the Mahāvaṃsa, chapter 5. There is one incident in this episode, which is of special interest. Once Tissa was out while a thera paid his daily visit to his father's house. The men in the house not finding any other seat, offered him the seat of Tissa. Tissa came back and saw the thera sitting on his own seat. He became angry and spoke to him in an unfriendly way. Thereupon the thera asked him, "Young man, dost thou know the mantra ?" Tissa asked the thera the same question. The thera replied, "Yes, I know." Then Tissa asked the thera to explain some knotty points in the Vedas. The thera expounded them and, in the end, asked Tissa a question from the Cittayamaka. Tissa was bewildered and asked the thera, "What mantra is that?" On the thera saying that it was Buddha-mantra, Tissa said, "Impart it to me." The thera said, "I impart it only to one who wears our robe." According to the Buddhaghosuppatti, one day a brahmin in the house of Kesī, father of Buddhaghosa, offered Buddhaghosa's seat to a thera who was Kesī's friend. This made Buddhaghosa angry and when the thera finished his meal, he asked him, "Bald-headed Sir, do you know the Vedas or are you acquainted with any other mantra?" The thera replied, "I know not only the Vedas but also another mantra," and then he rehearsed the three Vedas. Buddhaghosa then requested him to repeat his mantra. Thereupon the thera recited before him portions of the Abhidhammapiṭaka. Then knowing from the thera that it was Buddha-mantra and desiring to have a knowledge of that, he had his head shaven with the permission of his parents and became a monk.

The account in the Mahāvaṃsa differs from that in the Buddhaghosuppatti in one respect, namely, that Moggaliputta was asked questions from the Cittayamaka while Buddhaghosa was given Abhidhamma passages in relation to kusala, akusala, and avyākata dhamma. The Saddhamma-Samgaho which closely follows the Mahāvaṃsa, says that Buddhaghosa, too, was asked questions from the Cittayamaka (p. 52).

The stories in the Milinda Pañha, the Mahāvaṃsa and the Buddhaghosuppatti, are so alike that one cannot resist the temptation of saying that the author of the Buddhaghosuppatti, who must have been familiar with both the Milinda Pañha and the Mahāvaṃsa, borrowed the incidents from those works and grafted them on to his own.

CHAPTER III

ORIGIN AND DEVELOPMENT OF BUDDHIST COMMENTARIES

Nature of a commentary.

Before we proceed to give an account of the wonderful commentaries and other works for which we are indebted to Buddhaghosa, it will prove useful, we think, to discuss the important question as to the origin and development of Buddhist commentaries embodying exegesis, interpretation and explanation of the teachings of the Sage of the Śākyas. In the first place, however, a word or two about the nature of a commentary seems necessary. According to Indian tradition, a commentary means reading new meanings back into old texts according to one's own education and outlook. It explains the words and judgments of others as accurately and faithfully as possible and this remark applies to all commentaries, Sanskrit as well as Pāli. The commentary or bhāṣya, as it is called in Sanskrit, implies, of course, an amplification of a condensed utterance or expression which is rich in meaning and significance as the great Sanskrit poet, Māgha, says in his famous Kāvya[1]; but at the same time there is always an element of originality as the definition given by Bharata in his lexicography shows :—" Those

---

[1] "Saṁkhiptasyāpyatosyaiva vākyasyārthagarīyasaḥ
Suvistaratarāvācobhāṣyabhūtā bhavantu me."
(Śiśupālabadha, ii., 24.)

who are versed in the Bhāṣyas call that a Bhāṣya wherein the meaning of a condensed saying (sūtra) is presented in words that follow the text and where, moreover, the own words of the commentator himself are given."[1] We shall see in the account that we give below of the development of the commentary literature amongst the Buddhists that this method of giving their own words guided the great authors of the comments, although it was always adopted by way of expansion of an authoritative text.

Need for Buddhist Commentaries.

Before proceeding to discuss the question as to the origin of the Buddhist commentaries, we are confronted with the fact that the need for an accurate interpretation of the Buddha's words which formed the guiding principle of life and action of the members of the Sangha, was felt from the very first, even while the Master was living. Of course, there was at that time the advantage of referring a disputed question for solution to the Master himself and herein we meet with the first stage in the origin of the Buddhistic comments as we shall show below. All available evidence points to the fact that within a few years of the Buddha's enlightenment, Buddhist headquarters were established in places adjoining many important towns and cities of the time, viz: Benares, Rājagaha, Vesālī, Nālandā, Pāvā, Ujjenī, Campā, Uttara Madhurā, Ulumpā, Sāvatthī and so on. At each

---

[1] "Sūtrārtho varṇyate yatra padaiḥ sūtrānusāribhiḥ
Svapadāni ca varṇyante bhāṣyam bhāṣyavidoviduḥ.
Iti Liṅgādisaṁgrahaṭikāyāṁ Bharatah.
(Śabdakalpadruma.)

of these places there sprang up a community of Bhikkhus under the leadership and guidance of one or other of the famous disciples of the Buddha such as Māhakassapa, Māhakaccāyana, Mahākoṭṭhita, Sāriputta, Moggallāna. Following the rule of the wanderers or sophists, they used to spend the rainy season in a royal pleasure-garden or a monastery, and, thereafter, generally meet together once a year at Rājagaha, Veluvana, Sāvatthī or elsewhere. Friendly interviews among themselves, and occasional calls on contemporary sophists, were not unknown. Among these various leaders

Exchange of thought amongst the Buddha's early disciples.

of Bhikkhus, some ranked foremost in doctrine, some in discipline, some in analytical exposition, some in ascetic practices, some in story-telling, some in preaching, some in philosophy, some in poetry, and so on.[1] Among the Buddha's disciples and followers, there were men who came of Brahmin families, and who had mastered the Vedas and the whole of the Vedic literature. It may be naturally asked, "what were these profoundly learned and thoughtful Bhikkhus doing all the time?"

The Buddhist and Jaina texts tell us that the itinerant teachers of the time wandered about in the country, engaging themselves wherever they stopped in serious discussion on matters relating to religion, philosophy, ethics, morals and polity.[2] Discussions about the interpretation of

---

1 Vide Etadaggavaggo, Aṅguttara Nikāya I, p. 23 foll.; Mahāvaṁsa, edited by Geiger, '*The Council of Mahākassapa.*'

2 Vide my paper "A short account of the Wandering Teachers at the time of the Buddha." (J.A.S.B., New Series, Vol. XIV, 1918, No. 7.)

the abstruse utterances of the great teachers were frequent and the *raison dêtre* of the development of the Buddhist literature, particularly of the commentaries, is to be traced in these discussions. There are numerous interesting passages in the Tripiṭaka, telling us how from time to time contemporary events suggested manifold topics of discussion among the Bhikkhus, or how their peace was disturbed by grave doubts calling for explanations either from the Buddha himself or from his disciples. Whenever an interested sophist spoke vehemently 'in many ways in dispraise of the Buddha, in dispraise of the Doctrine and in dispraise of the Order'[1]; whenever another such sophist misinterpreted the Buddha's opinion,[2] whenever a furious discussion broke out in any contemporary Brotherhood,[3] or whenever a Bhikkhu behaved improperly, the Bhikkhus generally assembled under the pavilion to discuss the subject, or were exhorted by the Buddha or by his disciples to safeguard their interests. It was on one such occasion that the Buddha was led to offer an historical exposition of the moral precepts in accordance with his famous doctrine. "One should avoid all that is evil, and perform all that is good,"[4] that is to say, an explanation of the precepts in their negative and positive aspects. This is now incorporated in the first thirteen suttas of the Dīgha-Nikāya, and is familiarly known as the Sīlakkhandha—"The tract on morality"—lending its name to the first volume of

---

1 Dīgha Nikāya, Vol. I, Brahmajāla Suttanta, p. 1.

2 Majjhima Nikāya, III, pp. 207–8.

3 Majjhima Nikāya, II, Sāmagāmasutta, pp. 243–4.

4 "Sabba pāpassa akaranaṁ kusalassa upasampadā."

the Dīgha.[1] On another occasion Potaliputta, the wanderer, called on Samiddhi, and spoke thus, "According to Samaṇa Gotama, as I actually heard him saying, *Kamma* either by way of deed or by way of word is no *Kamma* at all, the real *Kamma* being by way of thought or volition only. For there is an attainment after having reached which one feels nothing (i.e. which transcends all sensible experience and pleasure and pain)." ["Moghaṁ kāyakammaṁ, moghaṁ vacikammaṁ, manokammaṁ eva saccaṁ ti; atthi ca sā samāpatti yaṁ samāpattiṁ samāpanno na kiñci vediyatīti."]

To him thus saying replied Samiddhi, "Speak not friend Potaliputta thus, speak not of him in this manner. Please do not misrepresent our teacher's point of view, for that is not good. He would never have said so."

"But tell me, friend Samiddhi, what a man will experience as the consequence of his deliberate action by way of thought, word and deed." "Pain," was the reply.[2]

Buddha's own exposition.

When a report of this discussion was submitted to the Buddha, he regretted that the muddle-headed Samiddhi had given such one-sided answer to the second point of the wanderer whom he had never met in his life. For, the right and complete answer would in that case have been that 'he will experience either pleasure or pain or neither pleasure nor pain.' But as regards Samiddhi's reply to the first point, he had nothing to say against it.

---

[1] See Dīgha Nikāya (P.T.S.), Vol. I.

[2] The rendering is not literal, though substantially faithful. Majjhima Nikāya, Vol. III, p. 207 foll.

Be that as it may, the fact remains that the wisdom and folly of Samiddhi, yet a young learner, formed the argument of the Buddha's longer analytical exposition of the all-important subject of *Kamma*, which is termed the *Mahākammavibhaṅga*,[1] in contradistinction to his shorter exposition, *the Cūlakamma-vibhaṅga*[2] which was addressed to a young Brahmin scholar named Subha. Thus it can be established that *the Mahākammavibhaṅga* was the Sutta basis of the Abhidhamma Exposition of the *Sikkhāpadavibhaṅga* which is incorporated in the second book of the Abhidhamma Piṭaka.[3] But, as a matter of fact, both these expositions have left their stamp on subsequent exegetical literature as is evidenced by the Nettipakarana and the Atthasālinī[4] and similar works. Scanning the matter more closely, we can say that Buddhaghosa's exposition of kamma in his Atthasālinī is really the meeting place of both.

The Majjhima Nikāya contains many other illuminating expositions of the Buddha, notably the Salāyatana Vibhaṅga,[5] the Araṇa Vibhaṅga,[6] the Dhātu Vibhaṅga[7] and the Dakkhinā Vibhaṅga, which have found their proper place in the Abhidhamma literature, supplemented by higher expositions. They have also found their way into the later commentaries including, of course, the monumental works of Thera Buddhaghosa. Then we have from Thera Sāriputta,

---

1 Majjhima Nikaya, III, pp. 207–215.

2 Ibid, III, pp. 202–206, Nettipakaraṇa, p. 182.

3 Vibhaṅga, pp. 285–292.

4 Atthasālinī, p. 64 foll.

5 Majjhima Nikāya, Vol. III, pp. 215–222.

6 Ibid., pp. 230–237.

7 Ibid., pp. 237–247.

8 Ibid., pp. 253–257.

the chief disciple of Buddha, a body of exposition of the four Aryan truths, the Saccavibhaṅga,[1] which had found its due place in the second book of the Abhidhamma Piṭaka, where it has been supplemented by a higher exposition (Abhidhammabhājaniya) based upon the sutta exposition. Sāriputta's exposition contains many of the stock-passages, or the older disconnected materials with which the whole of the Piṭaka literature, as we may reasonably suppose, was built up. This piece of independent commentary has been tacked on to the Satipaṭṭhāna Sutta, itself a commentary, and it furnishes the datum of a distinction between the Satipaṭṭhāna Sutta in the Majjhima Nikāya and the Mahāsatipaṭṭhāna Sutta in the Dīgha Nikāya.

Exposition of Sāriputta.

A complete catechism of important terms and passages of exegetical nature is ascribed to Sāriputta and is familiarly known as the Sangīti Suttanta[2] of which a Buddhist Sanskrit version exists in Tibetan and Chinese translations under the name of the Sangīti Parayāya Sūtra. The method of grouping various topics under numerical heads and of explaining by means of simple enumeration, invariably followed by Thera Sāriputta in the singularly interesting catechism referred to above, characterises two of the older collections, the Saṁyutta and the Aṅguttara and certain books of the Abhidhamma Piṭaka, notably the Puggala Paññatti, the materials of which were mostly drawn from the Aṅguttara

[1] Majjhima Nikāya, Vol. III, pp. 248–252.

[2] Dīgha Nikāya, III, p. 207 foll. See for references Prof. Tākākusu's highly instructive article on the Sarvāstivādins in J.P.T.S., 1905, p. 67.

Nikāya. This fact alone can bring home to us the nature of Sāriputta's work in connection with the Piṭaka literature. But Sāriputta does not exhaust the list. We have to consider other renowned and profoundly learned disciples of the Buddha, among whom some were women, who in their own way helped forward the process of development of the commentaries. Take for example, the case of Thera Mahākaccāyana who was allowed to enjoy the reputation of one who could give a detailed exposition of what was said by the Buddha in brief. The Majjhima Nikāya alone furnishes four exegetical fragments written by Mahākaccāyana,[1] which are of great value as forming the historical basis of three later works,[2] two in Pāli and one in Buddhist Sanskrit, which are all ascribed to him. The few fragments by Mahākaccāno (Mahākaccāyano) which have reached us, are important for another reason: they exhibit the working of the human mind in different directions. It is interesting to note that Mahākaccāno, so far as we can judge from these fragments, seldom indulges in mechanical enumeration and coining of technical terms as Sāriputta did. On the contrary, he confines himself to bringing out the inner significance and true philosophical bearing of the Buddha's first principles. The Gandhavaṁsa, a quite modern work written perhaps in the 17th century,[3] by Nandapañña of Burma, singles out Mahākaccāyana as the teacher who

Development of commentaries by other disciples—Mahākaccāyana.

---

1 Majjhima Nikāya, I, pp. 110 f.; III., pp. 78, 194 and 223.

2 viz: Nettipakaraṇa, Peṭakopadesa, Jñānaprasthāna Śāstra.

3 Mabel Bode, Pāli Literature of Burma, p. x.

not only took part in the First Council or explained from time to time the doctrines of the Buddha but compiled separate treatises.[1] Mahākaccāyana is mentioned as a teacher of Jambudvīpa, who was the chaplain (purohita) of King Candapradyota of Avanti, who had his capital at Ujjayinī.[2] The following exegetical works are attributed to the sage Mahākaccāyana:—

1. Kaccāyanagandho.
2. Mahāniruttigandho.
3. Cullaniruttigandho.
4. Nettigandho.
5. Peṭakopadesagandho.
6. Vaṇṇanītigandho.

Mahākoṭṭhita.

Then we have to make our acquaintance with Thera Mahākoṭṭhita who was regarded as an authority next to none but the Buddha himself on Paṭisambhidā or methodology of the Buddha's analytical system. In the Majjhima Nikāya again we meet with his disquisition on the characteristic marks or specific differences of current abstract terms signifying the various elements of experience.[3] He warns us at the same time against a possible misconception. Reason, understanding, perception, sensation and so forth are not entities. They are dissociated but all are inseparably associated[4] in reality.

---

[1] J.P.T.S., 1886, p. 59.

[2] Ibid., p. 66. : "Mahākaccāyano Jambudvīpikācariyo so hi Avantiraṭṭhe Ujjeninagare Candapaccotasa nāma rañño purohito hutvā....."

[3] Pajānāti pajānātīti .... tasmā paññavā ti vuccati .... Vijānāti vijānātīti .... tasmā viññānanti vuccati .... Majjhima Nikāya (P.T.S.) Vol. I, p. 292. [...."

[4] Majjhima Nikāya, Vol. I, p. 293 ".... Ime dhammā samsaṭṭhā no visaṃsaṭṭhā

The first part of Mahākoṭṭhita's explanation may be said to be the historical foundation of the Lakkhaṇahāra in the Nettipakaraṇa, of some passages in the Milinda-Pañho [1] and certain statements in the commentaries of Buddhaghosa [2]; we have similar contributions from Moggallāna, Ānanda, Dhammadinnā and Khemā, but we need not multiply instances.

The Abhidhamma as an exposition.

A careful examination of the contents of the second book of the Abhidhammapiṭaka proves beyond doubt that there is no hard and fast line between the Sutta and the Abhidhamma Piṭakas, the division resting mainly upon a difference in *modus operandi*. The Abhidhamma method was based upon and followed closely the line of the Sutta exposition, which is evidently earlier. It goes without saying that the difference between the two methods is not only one of degree, but at times, one of kind. In spite of the fact that the Abhidhamma exposition is direct, definite and methodical, we cannot say that in all cases, its value is greater than that of the Sutta exposition. There will always be a difference of opinion among Buddhist scholars as to whether the Abhidhamma books contain the genuine words of the Buddha Gotama.[3] It is nevertheless certain that the major portion of that literature is based upon the teachings and expositions of the Great Sage. There may be a Sariput-

---

1 Milinda-Pañho (Trenckner), p. 62.

2 e.g. Sumaṅgala-Vilāsinī, I, pp. 62–65.

3 See for a learned discussion on the subject among the Theras, Atthasālinī, pp. 29–31.

ta or some other unseen hands at work behind the scene, but, on the whole, the credit, as history proves it, belongs ultimately to the Buddha himself. The whole of the Abhidhamma Piṭaka has been separately classed by Buddhaghosa as Veyyākaraṇa or exposition. We are told that this class comprises also the gatha-less or prose suttas which are not found in the remaining eight classes of the early Buddhist literature.[1] The foregoing discussion has shown that the Vedallas need not be grouped as a separate class. There is no reason why the Cūlavedalla and the Mahāvedalla Suttas in the Majjhima Nikāya should not be included in the veyyākaraṇa class. At all events it has been clearly proved that in the Tripiṭakas, excluding the Kathāvatthu which was composed in the third century B.C., we have two layers, so to say, of veyyākaraṇa, viz. the Suttabhājanīya and the Abhidhammabhājanīya. Khandha, Vibhaṅga, Niddesa—these are but different synonyms of the same term. That is to say, the Suttas containing terminology, definition, enumeration or explanation, whether with or without such names as Khandha, Vibhaṅga, Niddesa, constitute the first great landmark; and the six Abhidhamma books, largely based upon the Suttas, the second landmark in the history of the Buddhist commentaries. The third landmark is not so easy to determine. Here we have a choice between a few works[2] ascribed

Two layers of veyyākarana in the early Buddhist literature.

[1] Atthasālinī, p. 26.

[2] Hardy, Introduction to the Nettipakaraṇa, p. xxxiii f.n. I. Kaccāyanapakaraṇaṁ, Mahāniruttipakaraṇam, Nettipakaraṇam, Cullaniruttí, Peṭakopadesa and Vaṇṇanīti.

to Mahākaccāno and the Kathāvatthu of which Thera Moggaliputta Tissa is said to be the author. As regards the date of the latter, it is certain that the book was composed about the time of the third Buddhist Council held under the auspices of King Aśoka. The case of Mahākaccāno's works is somewhat different. A careful survey of the Peṭakopadeso which is still buried in manuscripts, shows that whatever be the date of its composition, it is a supplementary treatise to the Nettipakaraṇa of which there is a beautiful edition in Roman character by Prof. E. Hardy. A Buddhist Sanskrit work, the Jñānaprasthāna Śāstra by a Mahākātyāyana, is held, as Prof. Tākākusu informs us, as an authoritative text by the Sarvāstivādins. This Śāstra is mentioned by Vasuvandhu in his Abhidharmakoṣa [1] as one of the seven Abhidhamma books. The work was translated into Chinese by Saṅghadeva and another in A.D. 383. Another translation was made in A.D. 657 by Hiuen Tsang who translated also the Abhidharmamahāvibhāsaśāstra, a commentary on Mahākātyāyana's work composed during the council under Kaniṣka. The Chinese traveller tells us that the Jñānaprasthāna Śāstra was composed three hundred years after the death of the Buddha. Buddhist scholars have yet to settle the question whether or not the Jñānaprasthāna has anything in common with the Nettipakaraṇa or with the Paṭṭhāna, the seventh book of the Abhidhammapiṭaka. The Netti, as we now have it, contains a section named Sāsanapaṭṭhāna which embodies a classification of the Piṭaka passages according to

The works of Mahākaccāyana.

[1] E. Burnouf's Introduction, p. 447.

their leading thoughts. Judging from the valuable extract from the Jñānaprasthāna given by Prof. Tākākusu we can decide once for all that the work is not identical with the Pāli Abhidhamma book, the Paṭṭhāna, though presumably it bears some relation to the latter. The Netti and the Jñānaprasthāna have many points in common, as they were written to serve a similar purpose.

In the opening paragraphs or pages of his two books, Mahākaccāyana frankly states that his work was not to start a new idea but to produce a systematic and analytical exposition of the expressions of others (paratoghosā). The Parikkhārahāra[1] of the Netti is a chapter based upon the Paṭṭhāna, though it throws new light on the subject of casual correlation. As appears from the section on Nayasamuṭṭhāna, Mahākaccāyana refers to the Buddhist schismatics or heretics (Diṭṭhicaritā asmim sāsane pabbajitā) whom he sharply distinguishes from the outsiders (Diṭṭhicaritā ito bahiddhāpabbajitā). Such a thing as this is not possible within the first century of the Buddha's Nibbāṇa. It presupposes the four Nikāyas and all other older books of the three piṭakas from which it has quoted several passages. Without going into further detail, we will not be far from the truth to assume that the works of Mahākaccāyana were indeed a connecting link between the Tripiṭaka on one side and all subsequent texts on the other. Thus if we have to choose between his works and the Kathāvatthu, the priority must be said to belong to the former.

---

[1] Nettipakaraṇa, pp. 78–80.

The Kathāvatthu.

The Kathāvatthu which is a Buddhist book of debate on matters of theology and philosophy, represents the fourth landmark. Buddhaghosa's plea for affiliation of this significant text to the Pāli Canon is ingenious enough. The Buddha laid down the main propositions which were discussed later by the adherents of different schools of thought.[1] It may, however, be doubted whether a book of controversy such as the Kathāvatthu, can be regarded as a landmark in the history of the commentaries. But a closer investigation will make it evident that this book of controversy is looked upon in one way as no more than a book of interpretation, as Mahākaccāyana[2] rightly points out that the Buddhist heretics, in spite of their individual differences, agreed so far as their regard for the teachings of the Master was concerned. The few specimens of controversy which the Kathāvatthu has embodied show that both sides referred to the Buddha as the final court of appeal. All have quoted passages from the Canon, though their interpretations differ widely.

The Milinda-Pañho.

Next we have to think of the "Questions of King Milinda" (Milinda-Pañho), which is a romantic dialogue between King Menander and Thera Nāgasena. It presupposes the Kathāvatthu and may be regarded philosophically as a richer synthesis of the isolated movements of Buddhist thought than the former.

The time when the Milinda-Pañho was composed may

---

[1] Atthasālinī, pp. 4–6.

[2] Nettipakaraṇa, p. 112.

be said to be the sixth landmark. Besides the Ceylon commentaries, Buddhaghosa has made casual references to the opinions of the Dīghabhānakas,[1] the Majjhimabhānakas[2] and other schools of Theras. In his introduction to the Sumaṅgalavilāsinī,[3] he gives us a short account of these schools of Theras, which were originally but so many schools of recitation rather than of opinion. In the background of Buddhaghosa's works which are catalogued here as the seventh landmark, there are the whole of Tripiṭaka, the works of Mahākaccāyana, the Kathāvatthu, the Milinda-Pañho,[4] the Paṇṇattivāda of teachers other than the Theravādins,[5] certain Vitaṇḍāvādins, Pakativāda[6] (the Sāṅkhya or the Yoga system), and the views of the Bhikkhus[7] of Ceylon.

The precursors of Buddhaghosa.

We have now to take into account another class of ancient Buddhist literature, the Porāṇas, of which our knowledge at present is based only upon some extracts in the Aṭṭhakathās.

The Porāṇas.

Nandapañña in his Gandhavaṁsa refers to the Porāṇācariyā or the ancient teachers. According to him, the five hundred Arahats who named the five Nikāyas, made their meanings and purports, their exposition and correction in the First council as well as the seven hundred Arahats who

[1] Atthasālinī, pp. 151, 399.
[2] Ibid., p. 420.
[3] Sumaṅgalavilāsinī, pp. 11–15.
[4] Atthasālinī, pp. 112, 114, 119, 120, 122, 142.
[5] Puggala Paññatti Commentary, P.T.S., pp. 173–175.
[6] Visuddhimagga, Vol. II, p. 525, ". . . . pakativādinaṁ pakativiya . . . ."
[7] See Sumaṅgalavilāsinī (P.T.S.), Vol. I, p. 1. Visuddhimagga, Vol. I (P.T.S.), pp. 36, 38.

made their proper interpretation, etc., in the Second council, together with one thousand Arahats who also made their proper interpretation in the Third council, are known as the Porāṇācariyā except Mahākaccāyana. It is distinctly stated in the Gandhavaṁsa that those who are the Porāṇācariyā are also the Aṭṭhakathācariyā or the teachers who wrote the Aṭṭhakathās.[1] Buddhaghosa speaks of the Porāṇā or the Porāṇakattherā[2] as persons who declare that those who observe the precepts will uphold the Buddhasāsana or the teaching of the Lord. This is said in connection with those who learn Dhamma from their teachers and maintain the views of their teachers. They do not entertain any dogmatic view of their own. These include, according to the Gandhavaṁsa, the Arahats who took part in the proceedings of the Three Councils and were evidently the earliest contributors to the commentary literature, as the name Aṭṭhakathācariyā given them by Nandapañña shows. The Mahāṭīkā also quotes from a Porāṇaṭṭhakathā as pointed out by Mrs. Rhys Davids.[3] We have seen before that questions often arose among the members of the Saṅgha about the interpretation of some of the utterances of the Buddha and they were at last submitted for decision to the Master himself while he was on earth but after his parinibbāṇa, the great and the revered teachers were approached. The interpretations given by them must have been consi-

1 J.P.T.S., 1886, Gandhavaṁsa, pp. 58–59.

2 Visuddhimagga (P.T.S.), p. 99 ".... ten'eva Porāṇakattherā: lajjī rakkhissati, lajjī rakkhissatīti tikkhattuṁ āhaṁsu."

3 Visuddhimagga, p. 764, note I.

dered decisive and valuable and hence they were no doubt preserved and when the commentaries came to be compiled, they were embodied in the great Aṭṭhakathās where they were simply referred to as the explanations given by the great teachers of old (Porāṇas). Buddhaghosa, when he quotes the Porāṇas, does so in a way that makes it probable that he is quoting the direct words of these ancient teachers as when he is quoting a canonical text. It is probable that the Porāṇaṭṭhakathās or the contributions made by these nameless sages of old, were preserved in the great Sinhalese commentaries and distinguished by being quoted in the original Pāli. Of course, in the absence of more definite data, we offer this as a mere suggestion. We are not inclined to agree with Mrs. Rhys Davids when she suggests[1] that these Porāṇas represented a consistent school of philosophical thought. Each teacher must have been responsible for himself alone and we think it hopeless to discover an organic connection among the numerous short and long passages attributed to the Porāṇas in Buddhaghosa's writings. They include matters of diverse interest and importance, metaphysical speculations as well as fanciful legends, as in the mythical account of the origin of the Licchavis in the Paramatthajotikā.[2] A collection of these Porāṇa citations will certainly be highly valuable, as Mrs. Rhys Davids suggests,[3] for the decision of matters connected with the history and development of Buddhist thought and Buddhist liter-

---

1 Visuddhimagga (P.T.S.), p. 768.

2 *Vide* my 'Kṣatriya clans in Buddhist India,' pp. 17-21.

3 Visuddhimagga, p. 764.

ature. We quote below a few of the many quotations made by Buddhaghosa of the views of the Porāṇas; it will be seen that they touch upon a variety of subjects. Thus in his Samantapāsādikā[1] while giving the history of the composition of the Vinaya-Aṭṭhakathā, Buddhaghosa says that this work was brought by Mahinda and others to Ceylon. From Mahinda and others, Ariṭṭhathera and others learnt and preserved it. From them up till now it has been preserved by their disciples from generation to generation.

After saying this in ordinary prose, he quotes the Porāṇas thus: "The Porāṇas say that on the full moonday of the month of Jyaiṣṭha, Mahinda and others including Iṭṭhiyo, Uttiyo, Bhaddasāla, Sambala, Sumaṇa sāmaṇero and Bhaṇḍuko upāsako assembled together and discussed whether it was proper time for them to go to Tambapaṇṇi (Ceylon)." [2]

The Porāṇas say that after living for thirty days on Vediyapabbata at Rājagaha, they thought that the time to go to Ceylon was come. So they went to Ceylon from Jambudvīpa and got down on the top of Ceṭiyapabbata.[3] Now it

---

1 Sinhalese Edition, U.P. Ekanāyaka, p. 30.

"Tass' attho ettāvatā pakāsito va hoti. Tatiya saṅgahato pana uddhaṁ imaṁ dīpaṁ Mahindādīhi ābhataṁ. Mahindato uggahetvā kiñci kālaṁ Ariṭṭhatherādīhi ābhataṁ. Tato yeva ajjatanā tesaṁ yeva antevāsika paraṁparābhatāya ācariya paraṁparāya ābhatanti veditabbam. Yathāhu 'Porāṇā." The Porāṇas also speak of the same thing in verses.

2 "Mahindo nāma nāmena Saṁghathero tadā ahū,
Iṭṭhiyo Uttiyo thero Bhaddasālo ca Sambalo
Sāmaṇero ca Sumano chaḷabhiñño mahiddhiko
Bhaṇḍuko sattamo tesañ diṭṭhasacco upāsako
Iti ete mahānāgā mantayiṁsu rahogatāti."

Cf. Dīpavaṁsa (Oldenberg), p. 62, lines 24-25 and p. 63 line 1.

3 Samantapāsādikā, Sinhalese Edition, p. 35.

will be seen that the Porāṇa account is in verse and furnishes greater details of the same historical event, and evidently it forms the basis of the prose account. In all probability, while translating the account from the Sinhalese Aṭṭhakathā, Buddhaghosa found the Porāṇa verses there just as we have them now in the original Pāli and simply transferred them to his commentary without having to change the language. It will be observed that these verses are the same as those given in the Mahāvaṁsa and apparently the Aṭṭhakathā and the chronicle drew from the same source.

Again in his Visuddhimagga, Buddhaghosa quotes a verse from the Porāṇas, giving an explanation of a term, thus: "The Porāṇas say, 'Bhagavā' means the great (Seṭṭho), Bhagavā means the best (Uttama) and as he is endowed with honour and respect, therefore he is called Bhagavā."[1]

In the same work he quotes another Porāṇa verse with reference to a point of discipline of the Bhikkhus, thus: "The Porāṇas say, the following points are to be considered in a case of theft committed by a Bhikkhu: the thing stolen, time, country, price and also the period for which the thing stolen had been used by the real owner."[2]

"Vediyagirimhi Rājagahe vasitvā timsarattiyo,
Kālova gamanassāti gacchāma dīpamuttaṁ.
Phalinā Jaṁbudīpato hamsarājā va ambare
Evaṁuppattitā therā nipatiṁsu naguttame.
Purato puraseṭṭhassa pabbate meghasannibhe,
Patiṁsu Sīlakūṭamhi hamsāvanagamuddhani."

[1] Samantapāsādikā, p. 62. Cf. Visuddhimagga (P.T.S.), p. 209.
"Bhagavā ti vacanaṁ seṭṭhaṁ Bhagavā ti vacanuttamaṁ,
Garugāravayutto so Bhagavā tena vuccatiti."

[2] Ibid., p. 177

Next, we quote from his Atthasālinī a Porāṇa passage giving details about mythical regions, thus: " The Porāṇas say that Pāṭali, Simbali, Jambu and Pāricchattaka of the Devas, Kadamba, Kapparukkha and Sirīsena—these seven trees are existing in Asuraloka, among the garuḷas, in the Aparagoyāna, in Uttarakuru, in Pubbavideha and in the Tāvatiṁsa Heaven respectively." [1]

Conclusion.

To sum up: we have seen that there is evidence enough to confirm the truth of the tradition that neither Buddhaghosa, nor the Thera Mahinda, nor the theras of old, were the originators of the commentaries. We may say that the Buddha himself, his immediate disciples and their disciples, all prepared the way for the great Buddhaghosa; at the same time we cannot agree with those who totally deny the latter's claim to any originality. The Niddesa which is an old commentary on certain suttas in the Sutta Nipāta, cannot compare favourably with Buddhaghosa's Paramatthajotikā.

" Vatthuṁ kālañca desañca agghaṁ paribhogapañcanaṁ
Tulayitvā pañcaṭhānāni dhāreyyatthaṁ vicakkhaṇo."
Atthasālinī (P.T.S.), p. 299.

[1] " Pāṭali simbaḷi jambu devānaṁ pāricchattako
kadambo kapparukkho ca sirīsena bhavati sattamanti."

CHAPTER IV

BUDDHAGHOSA'S WORKS

The Mahāvaṁsa tells us, as we have seen in Chapter I, that before Buddhaghosa left India for Ceylon under the instructions of his spiritual preceptor, the sage Revata Thera, he had already produced the Ñānodaya and the Atthasālinī. The Ñānodaya (Sanskrit Jñānodaya), as its name, 'Rising of Knowledge,' implies, is a philosophical treatise, about the exact nature of the contents of which we know nothing as yet, as it does not appear to have been preserved; nor is any description of this early work of Buddhaghosa to be met with anywhere in Pāli literature. The preservation of it was not perhaps considered necessary as his later and more informed work, the Visuddhimagga, had most probably incorporated everything of a permanent value that was in it and thereby supplanted it.

The Ñānodaya.

The Ceylonese chronicle further tells us that Buddhaghosa wrote also the Atthasālinī or commentary on the Dhammasaṅgaṇi before his departure for the southern island and the Sāsanavaṁsa supports this statement.

The Atthasālinī.

The Buddhaghosuppatti has got nothing to say about

[1] Buddhaghoso ca āyasmato Revatassa santike nisīdanto Ñānodayaṁ nāma gandhaṁ Atthasāliniṁ ca gandhaṁ akāsi. Tatopacchā parittaṭṭhakathaṁ kattukāmo hutvā ārabhi. (Sāsanavaṁsa, P.T.S., p. 31.)

this work. But the Saddhamma Sangaho[1] has an interesting account of it. "Buddhaghosa while travelling in Jambudvīpa, came to a vihāra where the Mahāthera Revata dwelt. There he began writing the Atthasālinī, a commentary on the Dhammasaṅgaṇi, after completing the Ñānodaya. The revered Thera Revata seeing him thus engaged, spoke to him thus, 'O Buddhaghosa, in Jambudvīpa, there is only the text of the three piṭakas. The commentaries (Aṭṭhakathās) and the opinions of the teachers (Ācariyavādā) do not exist here. The Aṭṭhakathās have been recited in the three convocations made by Sāriputta and others and translated into Sinhalese by Mahinda. They exist in Ceylon. Go there and render all into Māgadhi.'" With reference to the same work, we are further told: "Buddhaghosa immediately after having rendered the Mahāpaccariyaṭṭhakathā which occurs in the Abhidhammapiṭaka from Sinhalese into Māgadhi, composed the commentary (Aṭṭhakathā) on the Dhammasaṅgaṇi, named the Atthasālinī."[2]

In the first statement we are told that the work was produced at Gayā before Buddhaghosa proceeded to Ceylon and this is what we find in the Mahāvaṁsa; whereas in the second, we are told that it was written after several other works had been produced. These two apparently contradictory statements are no doubt to be reconciled, as Mrs. Rhys Davids suggests,[3] by thinking that the Atthasālinī, though at first written at Gayā, was subjected to a thorough revision by its author after his studies in the great Aṭṭha-

[1] J.P.T.S., 1890, p. 53. [2] Ibid., 1890, p. 56.
[3] Mrs Rhys Davids A Buddhist Manual of Psychological Ethics, p. xxi.

kathās in Ceylon. This would be quite natural in the case of a commentary dealing with abstruse philosophical theses. The Saddhamma Sangaho further gives us the information that Buddhaghosa, while revising this commentary, derived his materials from the Mahā Paccarī or the Great Raft commentary which probably contained a more detailed exposition of the subject matter dealt with here. In the introductory verses to his Atthasālinī, quoted in Chapter I, we have seen that the author refers to the Aṭṭhakathās which he had translated into the pure language of Magadha. Further, in the body of the work he quotes from or refers to, as Mrs. Rhys Davids has shown, many works including the Ceylonese Aṭṭhakathās and some of his own works, such as the Samantapāsādikā and the Visuddhimagga. Evidently, therefore, the whole book was re-written in the light of the additional knowledge he acquired in Ceylon. The text of the Atthasālinī has been edited by Dr. Edward Müller for the Pāli Text Society of England and an excellent translation has come out due to the combined labours of Mrs. Rhys Davids and Mr. Maung Tin, so that this commentary of the Thera Buddhaghosa is now available to everyone who is interested in it.

The Visuddhimagga.

Before speaking of the other great commentaries, we shall refer to the Visuddhimagga which is esteemed as an Encyclopædia of Buddhism. That the Visuddhimagga[1] (Path of Purity) was

[1] Mr. Nagai in the Journal of the Pāli Text Society, points out that the Visuddhimagga of Buddhaghosa is but a revised version of Vimuttimagga by a thera named Upatissa of Ceylon. He also points out that the author, Upatissa, belonged

Buddhaghosa's first production in Ceylon is beyond dispute. He does not quote from or refer to any of his other works, as is the case with the Atthasālinī, but it must have been produced after he had gone to Ceylon, as is evident from the fact that he refers to the Aṭṭhakathās which were available in Ceylon only and not on the main-land. It is said to have been composed 'under somewhat romantic circumstances.'[1] 'It is called a marvellous production.' It has earned for its author an everlasting fame. It is considered to be the only book in which the whole of the Buddhist system is well depicted. It does not contribute anything to the Piṭakas but it aims at a systematic arrangement of their contents.[2] "It is not a commentary on any text, but claims to be a compendium of the whole Buddha-system, conduct, meditation, contemplation, the elements of being, the senses, the truths, the chain of causation and the rest."[3] The character and contents of the Visuddhimagga have been thus described by Spence Hardy: "The Visuddhimagga, a compendium formed by Buddhaghosa, presents an abstract of the doctrinal and metaphysical parts of the Buddhistical creed,

---

to the first century A.D., and was a contemporary of King Vasabha of Ceylon (A.D. 66–109). The work is entirely lost in Ceylon and it exists only in a Chinese translation dated A.D. 505 by a Cambodian priest named Saṅghapāla. Mr. Nagai in Section 5 of his article shows how the Chinese text agrees generally with the text of the Visuddhimagga, and further records thus, "the difference in each case can be accounted for in one way or another on the ground of re-arrangement, interpolation or curtailment. On the whole, the description of the Chinese is much simpler than that of the Pāli." (J.P.T.S., 1917–1919, pp. 69–80.)

1 See chapters I and II.

2 Buddhism, Primitive and Present, by Copleston, p. 213.

3 Ibid., p. 212.

which, as being the work of the last commentator on the Buddhistical scriptures, acquires an authority and authenticity which no compendium exclusively formed by any Orientalist of a different faith, and more modern times, can have any claim to . . . . ."[1]

An account of the contents of the Visuddhimagga is recorded in the Sumaṅgala-Vilāsinī which runs thus, " The nature of the sīlakathā, dhūtadhammā, kammaṭṭhānāni together with all the cariyāvidhāni, jhānāni, the whole scope of the samāpatti, the whole of abhiññāna, the exposition of the paññā, the khandha, the dhātu, the āyatanāni, indiriyāni, the four ariyasaccāni, the pachchayākārā, the pure and comprehensive nayā and the indispensable maggā and viphassanabhāwanā."

Mr. Gray in his appreciation of this work remarks, " If he had written nothing else, it alone would have secured him undying fame."[2]

Contents of the Visuddhimagga.

Let us go into the contents of the work as briefly as possible. The first chapter deals with nidānakathā, sīlaniddeso and five kinds of sīla ; the second chapter, with dhutaṅganiddeso ; the thirteen dhutaṅgas (name of certain ascetic practices) are discussed here ; the third chapter deals with kammaṭṭhānagahaṇaniddeso. It explains how to begin meditation. The fourth chapter deals with paṭhavikasiṇaniddeso ; in it are described eighteen faults (kasiṇadosas) which render a vihāra unfit, two grades of samādhi and so

[1] Spence Hardy, Manual of Buddhism, p. 531-532.

[2] James Gray, Buddhaghosuppatti, Introduction, p. 31.

forth. The fifth chapter deals with sesakasiṇaniddeso. Mr. Warren in his table of contents of Buddhaghosa's Visuddhimagga has named Chapter V as dasakasiṇa-niddeso (Exposition of ten Kasiṇas).[1] The sixth chapter treats of asubha kammaṭṭhāna-niddeso. In it we have the description of the asubhas and the use of them The seventh chapter is devoted to cha-anussati-niddeso; under this we have ten anussatis and three lokas. The eighth chapter treats of anussatikammaṭṭhāna-niddeso. We have contemplation of death, eightfold manasikāravidhi, etc. The ninth chapter deals with brahmavihāra-niddeso, classes of persons unsuitable, various directions for removal of enmity. The tenth chapter deals with āruppa-niddeso; here we have the exposition of the four āruppas. The eleventh chapter explains samādhi-niddeso. Samādhi, the five blessings of samādhi, etc., are dealt with in this chapter. The twelfth and the thirteenth chapters deal with iddhi-vidhā-niddeso and abhiññā-niddeso. The remaining chapters deal with khandhaniddeso, āyatanadhātuniddeso, indriya-sacca-niddeso, paññābhūmi-niddeso, diṭṭhivisuddhi-niddeso, kaṅkhāvitaraṇavisuddhi-niddeso, maggāmaggañāṇa-dassanavisuddhi-niddeso, Paṭipadā-ñāṇadassanavisuddhi-niddeso, Ñāṇadassanavisuddhi-niddeso, Paññābhāvanānisaṁsa-niddeso.

In short, the work deals with kusala, akusala, avyākata dhamma, āyatana, dhātu, satipaṭṭhānas, kammas, pakati, and many other topics of Buddhist philosophy. It contains the whole of the Buddhist philosophy in a nut-shell. The

[1] J.P.T.S., 1891-1893, p. 97.

language of the Visuddhimagga is very difficult to understand. The vocabulary is very rich. Big words are often used and long passages are frequent. It is complete in itself. It was written at the request of the Thera Saṅghapāla.[1] The Visuddhimagga is an abridged compilation of the three piṭakas together with quotations from the Aṭṭhakathās on those passages of the three piṭakas which are mentioned in it. ("Buddhaghoso ca saddhiṁ aṭṭhakathāya piṭakattayaṁ saṁkhipitvā Visuddhimaggaṁ akāsi." Sāsanavaṁsa, p. 31.) According to Mr. E. W. Burlingame, the approximate date of the Visuddhimagga is 410 A.D.[2]

The Ceylonese commentaries on works of the Tripiṭaka.

We now come to the great commentaries on works of the Tripiṭaka for the production of which Buddhaghosa crossed the sea. We have already referred to the story of his voyage to Ceylon. A portion of it will well bear repetition. His teacher Revata is represented as saying to him, "The Pāli (text of the Tripiṭaka) only has been brought over here, no commentary is extant in this place. The divergent opinions of the teachers other than the Theravādins do not likewise exist. The Ceylon commentary, which is faultless, and which was written in Sinhalese by the thoughtful Mahinda with due regard to the methods of exposition as taught by the supreme Buddha, put up before the three councils, and rehearsed by Sāriputta and others, is current among the people of Ceylon. Please go there and study it, and then

---

1 Sāsanavaṁsa, p. 30, "Saṁghapālatherassa āyācanaṁ ārabbha Visuddhimaggo kato."

2 Buddhist Legends (Harvard Oriental Series). Pt. I, p. 48.

translate it into Māgadhi which will be useful to the world."[1] From this it is evident that the commentaries were not to be found in India at the time of Buddhaghosa: they were all to be found in Ceylon. It follows further that the commentaries, as they have come down to us, were not the original compositions of either Buddhaghosa or his illustrious predecessor Mahinda. These commentaries, as appears from tradition, were originally the productions not of a single author but of a community of brethren. Mahinda was merely a translator into Sinhalese, and Buddhaghosa, a retranslator into Pāli. Buddhaghosa himself frankly admits in his prologues to several commentaries[2] that he annotated those passages only which were not commented upon by his predecessors, and the rest he only translated. We are told by the Mahāvaṁsa as well as the later works on Buddhaghosa's life how the great thera after his arrival in Ceylon had to submit to an examination which resulted in the production of the

---

[1] Mahāvaṁsa (Turnour), p. 251. "Pālimattaṁ idhānitam, n'atthi Aṭṭhakathā idha, | tathācariyavādā ca bhinnarūpā na vijjare, | Sīhalaṭṭhakathā suddhā Mahindena matimatā saṅgītittayaṁ ārūḷhaṁ sammāsaṁbuddhadesitaṁ | Sāriputtādigītañ ca kathāmaggaṁ samekkhiya | katā sīhalabhāsāya sīhalesu pavattati. | Taṁ tattha gantvā sutvā tvaṁ Māgadhānaṁ niruttiyā | parivattehi, sā hoti sabbalokahitāvahā."

Cf. Sāsanavaṁsa, p. 31. It explains 'bhinnarūpā na vijjare' as bhinnohutvā atthi, which is a misinterpretation. "Jambudīpe . . . . pāḷimattaṁ yeva atthi, aṭṭhakathā pana natthi. Aṭṭhakathā tīsu ca saṁgītīsu ārūḷhā pāḷiyo Sāriputtatherādīhi desito "Kathāmaggo" Sīhaladīpe atthi."

[2] Sumaṅgala-Vilāsinī, Vol. I (P.T.S.), p. 1.

". . . . therānaṁ theravamsappadīpānaṁ
sunipuṇavinicchayānaṁ Mahāvihārādivāsīnaṁ
Hitvā punappunāgataṁ atthaṁ attham pakāsayissāmi."
Cf. Sāratthapakāsini (MSS.), p. 1.

Visuddhimagga, and in the final granting of permission to the Indian scholar to use all the Sinhalese commentaries. The Saddhamma-Sangaho narrates how the revered Buddhaghosa took all the books and, while dwelling at the Padhānaghara on the southern side of the Mahāvihāra, translated all the Sinhalese commentaries into Māgadhi.[1] The Sāsanavaṁsa says that more than nine hundred and thirty years since the passing away of the Lord, during the reign of the Burmese King, Sañ-Lañ-Kroṁ, Buddhaghosa wrote his works.[2] The Aṭṭhakathās which existed at the time Buddhaghosa lived in Ceylon, are no longer extant, but the names of some of them have come down to us mainly in Buddhaghosa's own works which supplanted them elsewhere. These names as given by Mrs. Rhys Davids are: "(1) The commentary of the dwellers in the 'North Minster'—the Uttara Vihāra—at Anurādhapura. (2) The Mūla, or Mahā-Aṭṭhakathā, or simply 'The Aṭṭhakathā' of the dwellers in the 'Great Minster'—the Mahā Vihāra—also at Anurādhapur. (3) The Andha-aṭṭhakathā, handed down at Kāñcipura (Conjevaram) in South India. (4) The Mahā Paccarī or Great Raft, said to be so called from its having been composed on a raft somewhere in Ceylon. (5) The Kurunda Aṭṭhakathā so called because it was composed at the Kurundavelu Vihāra in Ceylon. (6) The Sankhepa

[1] Saddhamma-Sangaho, p. 55. "Buddhaghoso sabbe potthake gahetvā Mahavihārassa dakkhiṇa-bhāge Padhānagharaṁ nāma ekasmin pāsāde vasanto sabbaṁ Sīhalaṭṭhakathaṁ parivattetvā mūlabhāsāya Māgadhikāya niruttiyā ......"

[2] Sāsanavaṁsa (P.T.S.), p. 73. "Bhagavato pana parinibbānato tiṁsādhikānaṁ navavassasatānaṁ upari Marammaraṭṭhe Sañ-Lañ-Kroṁ nāmena raññā samakālavasena... Buddhaghoso Buddhadattatherehi ..... te te gandhe akaṁsu."

Aṭṭhakathā or short commentary, which, as being mentioned together with the Andha commentary, may possibly be also South Indian."

Of these, Buddhaghosa's Samantapāsādikā mentions three, as we have seen, viz: the Mahā-Aṭṭhakathā, the Mahāpaccarī-aṭṭhakathā and the Mahākurunda-aṭṭhakathā.

Coming now to the individual works of Buddhaghosa's commentaries on the Tripiṭaka, we find, first of all, his commentaries on the Vinaya Piṭaka which may be described thus:

Commentaries on the Vinaya Piṭaka—the Samantapāsādikā.

1. Samantapāsādikā—It was written at the request of a thera named Buddhasiri. It is a voluminous commentary on the five books of the Vinaya Piṭaka. In the preface to this work, the commentator tells us that this was the first commentary he wrote on the canonical texts. He apologises for undertaking to write, first of all, a commentary on the Vinaya Piṭaka, contrary to the usual order of Dhamma and Vinaya. He says that Vinaya is the foundation of the Buddhist faith. The work itself supplies us with sufficient materials with which to write a social, political, moral, religious and philosophical history of ancient India. The rules of morality are well explained in it. The Samantapāsādikā was followed by commentaries on the four Nikāyas in succession which preceded the commentaries on the seven books of the Abhidhamma Piṭaka. The book can be had in three volumes in Burma Some printed portions are avail-

[1] A Buddhist Manual of Psychological Ethics by C. A. F. Rhys Davids, p. xxii.

able in Ceylon. A portion of the Pāli Samantapāsādikā was rendered into Chinese by Sanghabhadra in 489 A.D.[1]

The Kaṅkhāvitaraṇi.

2. Kaṅkhāvitaraṇī—He wrote it of his own accord and not at the instance of others. It is a commentary on the Pātimokkha (which is one of the books of the Vinaya Piṭaka) and embodies certain rules of discipline (Vinaya) which can easily be committed to memory by Bhikkhus and Bhikkhunis. It is available in Ceylon, Siam, Burma and England. We have in manuscript an ancient sinhalese glossary on the Kaṅkhāvitaraṇī preserved in the Government Oriental Library, Colombo. The date of the work is between 410 A.D. and 432 A.D.[2]

Buddhaghosa also wrote commentaries on the various books of the Sutta Piṭaka :—

Commentaries on the Sutta Piṭaka—the Sumaṅgalavilāsinī.

1. Sumaṅgalavilāsinī—It was written at the request of the Saṅghathera Dāṭha. It is a commentary on the Dīgha-Nikāya (Long Discourse) which is divided into three parts :—

(1) Sīlakkhandha.

(2) Mahāvagga.

(3) Patheya or Pāṭikavagga.

In the Sumaṅgalavilāsinī, we have a vivid picture of sports and pastimes, geographical position of countries, effects of the life of a recluse, etc., in ancient days. The most essential points of Buddhism, the details of Arahatship, are not only described in full but also compared with the

[1] See Nariman's Literary History of Sanskrit Buddhism, p. 263.

[2] A Catalogue of Pāli, Sinhalese and Sanskrit Manuscripts in the temple libraries of Ceylon compiled by the late Louis De Zoysa, Colombo, 1885, p. 2.

Brahman ideal on the one hand and with the ordinary morality of a good layman on the other. It is rich in historical information and folk-lore and it abounds in narratives which throw a flood of light on the social, political, religious and philosophical history of India at the time of the Buddha. It has been printed and published in Burma. Two sermons of it in two parts have been published in Ceylon. It gives us a glimpse of the erudite learning of Buddhaghosa. Its language is not so confused as that of his other commentaries.

The Papañcasūdanī.

2. Papañcasūdanī—It was written at the request of a thera named Buddhamitta. It is a commentary on the Majjhima Nikāya (Middle Discourse) which is divided into three parts:—

(1) Mūlapaññāsa
(2) Majjhimapaññāsa and
(3) Uparipaññāsa.

In Ceylon the first fifty sermons and one or two sermons of the Majjhimapaññāsa have been published in several parts.

The Sāratthapakāsinī.

3. Sāratthapakāsinī—It was written at the request of a thera named Jotipāla. It is a commentary on the Samyutta Nikāya, that is to say, a commentary on

(1) Sagāthavagga,
(2) Nidānavagga,
(3) Khandhavagga,
(4) Saḷāyatanavagga and
(5) Mahāvagga.

The whole book can be had in print in Ceylon and Burma.

4. Manorathapūraṇī—It was written at the request of a thera named Bhaddanta. It is a commentary on the Aṅguttara Nikāya which is divided into eleven parts, such as, Ekanipāta, Dukanipāta, Tikanipāta, etc. The complete work has been printed and published in Ceylon and Burma.

The Manorathapūraṇī.

5. Khuddakanikāyaṭṭhakathā—Buddhaghosa wrote a commentary on four books of the Khuddaka Nikāya. He wrote commentaries on the Khuddakapāṭha, the Dhammapada, and the Suttanipāta. Commentaries on the Khuddakapāṭha and on the Suttanipāta are known as the Paramatthajotikā. He wrote them of his own accord. They have recently been edited and published by the Pāli Text Society, London.

The Khuddakanikāyaṭṭhakathā.

Next we come to the Dhammapadaṭṭhakathā. Doubts have been raised whether Buddhaghosa is the author of this work. It is a work of immense bulk consisting not merely of the Aṭṭhakathā proper, that is, explanations of the words and expressions in the text, but also an immense mass of illustrative tales of the nature of the Jātaka stories. H. C. Norman who has edited the complete work for the P.T.S., is of opinion that these illustrative stories are from the hand of a later redactor and the word for word commentary only is due to Buddhaghosa; while Mr. E. W. Burlingame in his Buddhist Legends translated from the

The Dhammapadaṭṭhakathā.

Dhammapada commentary, would not attribute even this much of the authorship to the great commentator. According to Buddhist tradition, Buddhaghosa is the author of this Aṭṭthakathā and this is supported by the colophon of the work itself which attributes it to him. There is also a reference to the Mahāvihāra in Ceylon, as Norman points out,[1] and this fact also would support its connection with Buddhaghosa, as it was here that Buddhaghosa wrote his commentaries. Mr. Burlingame lays the greatest stress upon the difference in language and style between the Dhammapadaṭṭhakathā and the other commentaries which undoubtedly belong to Buddhaghosa. But here we may suggest that the difference that is observable, may be due to the difference in the subject-matter of the various texts taken up for comment. The Dhammapada, unlike the great Nikāyas which consist of prose and gāthās, is entirely made up of gāthās with the prose setting, which, in the Nikayas, is supplied in the text itself. Here, therefore, there was the necessity of bringing it into line with those canonical works. Hardy has pointed out[2] that the story of the merchant Ghosaka, as told by Buddhaghosa in the Manorathapūraṇī, differs from the same story as told in the Dhammapada commentary. Here we must bear in mind the fact that Buddhaghosa was not writing an independent commentary of his own on the canonical texts, but that he was, for the most part, translating or compiling from various Sinhalese commentaries, sometimes from the

[1] Dhammapadaṭṭhakathā, (P.T.S.) Vol. I, pt. 2, p. xvii.
[2] J.R.A.S., 1898, pp. 741-794.

Mahā-Aṭṭhakathā, sometimes from the Mahāpaccarī and sometimes again from the Kurunda Aṭṭhakathā; Buddhaghosa, therefore, cannot be held responsible for the variations in the narratives, which might have been due to the differences in the authorship of the great old commentaries which, as we have shown in the last chapter, embodied the joint labours of an immense number of Buddhist sages and scholars who had been working at the interpretation of the Master's sayings ever since they were uttered; and the commentaries had been growing through the many centuries that intervened between the Buddha and our commentator who gave the final shape to them. Some difference in the large number of legends, fables and stories incorporated in the commentaries, may naturally be expected. We are, therefore, inclined to think that the colophon ascribing the authorship of the Dhammapada-aṭṭhakathā to Buddhaghosa is correct, though this authorship so far as the Dhammapada commentary is concerned, might have extended to no more than translating from the original commentaries in Ceylon. That there were different versions of the illustrative stories as well as the recensions of the Dhammapada itself before Buddhaghosa, appears from a comparison of the Pāli work with the Chinese translation, the text of which is said to have been taken to China in 223 A.D. Beal's 'Dhammapada from the Buddhist Canon'[1] translated from the Chinese version, shows a great deal of difference from the Pāli work in the canonical gāthās as well as the illustrative tales. Therefore, the differences observed in the two versions

[1] Norman, The commentary on the Dhammapada, Vol. I, pt. II, pp. xv–xvi.

of the story of Ghosaka in the two commentaries of Buddhaghosa are not of much consequence.

In the prologue of the Dhammapada-aṭṭhakathā, Buddhaghosa says that he translated the Sinhalese commentaries into Māgadhi (tanti), adding here and there notes of his own at the request of a thera named Kumārakassapa.[1] The Dhammapada commentary contains many humorous tales, animal stories, legends of saints, etc. Some of these stories are referred to in the Milinda-Pañho, e.g. Maṭṭhakuṇḍali, Sumaṇa, etc. (vide Buddhist Legends, pt. I, pp. 60–62). Parallels to the stories of this book can be found in the Divyāvadāna and in the Tibetan Kandjur (vide Buddhist Legends, pt. I, pp. 63–64).

Buddhaghosa's commentaries on the Abhidhamma Piṭaka are the following:—

Commentaries on the Abhidhamma Piṭaka.

1. Atthasālinī—A commentary on a certain section of the Dhammasaṅgaṇi, about which we have already spoken at some length. In Burma, it is widely studied by student monks and is often quoted by authors of Abhidhamma works. It is one of the best known works of Buddhaghosa. A cursory

[1] Dhammapada commentary (P.T.S.), edited by Norman, Vol. I, pp. 1–2.

"....nipuṇā Atthavaṇṇanā,
Yā Tambapaṇṇīdīpamhi dīpabhāsāya saṇṭhitā,
........dantena samacārinā
Kumārakassapenāhaṁ therena........
........abhiyācito,
....aropayitvāna tantibhāsaṁ manoramaṁ,
gāthānaṁ vyañjanapadaṁ yaṁ tattha na vibhāvitaṁ,
kevalaṁ taṁ vibhāvetvā sesaṁ taṁ eva atthato,
bhāsantarena bhāsissaṁ āvahanto vibhāvinaṁ,
manaso pītipāmojjaṁ atthadhammūpanissitanti."

examination of the Atthasālinī shows that it was composed after the Samantapāsādikā to which it refers in pages 97 and 98 of the P.T.S. edition.

2. Sammohavinodanī—A commentary on the Vibhaṅga (Exposition).

3. Dhātukathāpakaraṇaṭṭhakathā—A commentary on the Dhātukathā (talk of elements).

4. Puggala Paññattipakaraṇaṭṭhakathā—A commentary on the Puggala Paññatti, an English translation of which by the present writer is being printed and published by the Pāli Text Society, London.

5. Kathāvatthu aṭṭhakathā—A commentary on the Kathāvatthu (Points of controversy).

6. Yamakapakaraṇaṭṭhakathā—A commentary on the Yamaka.

7. Paṭṭhānapakaraṇaṭṭhakathā--A commentary on the Paṭṭhāna, the last book of the Abhidhamma Piṭaka, written at the request of a monk named Cullabuddhaghosa.[1]

Buddhaghosa also wrote the Paritta-aṭṭhakathā which is one of the books of the Abhidhamma Piṭaka. His later commentaries refer to his earlier ones[2] and all presuppose his Visuddhimagga.[3]

---

[1] According to the Gandhavaṁsa (J.P.T.S., 1886, p. 63), an author named Cullabuddhaghosa composed two treatises, Jātattaginidānaṁ and Sotattaginidānaṁ. It appears that he flourished long after Buddhaghosa. The Gandhavaṁsa gives the names of a number of authors between him and Buddhaghosa. He must, therefore, be differentiated from Cullabuddhaghosa referred to here.

[2] Sumaṅgalavilāsinī, Vol. I, p. 70, "Atthikehi Samantapāsādikaṁ Vinayaṭṭhakathaṁ oloketvā gahetabbaṁ." Puggala Paññatti commentary, p. 222, "Ayam Aṅguttaraṭṭhakathāyaṁ nayo." See also P.P. Com., p. 247. Atthasālinī refers to the Samantapāsādikā, pp. 97 and 98, to the Vibhaṅga commentary, p. 407.

[3] Atthasālinī, pp. 168, 186, 187, 190, 198. Sumaṅgalavilāsinī, Vol. I, p. 2;

Besides these commentaries, it is recorded in the Sāsanavaṁsa, Buddhaghosa wrote Piṭakattayalakkhaṇagandha; and a Sanskrit work, "Padyacūḍāmaṇi"[1] attributed to Buddhaghosa, has been recently published by order of the Government of Madras. It has been edited by Mr. Kuppuswāmi Śāstrī and another. It is a mahākāvya in Sanskrit on the life of the Buddha. There is nothing in the book itself to show who the author was except only a few words of usual modesty in the second and third stanzas of the first canto. The colophons at the end of the cantos describe the work as written by Buddhaghoṣācārya or simply Buddhaghosa. Mr. S. Kuppuswāmi Śāstrī, the editor of the work, has identified this Buddhaghosa with the great commentator. Before discussing the question of this identity we shall give a summary of its contents which will put us in a position to examine the matter thoroughly. The work consists of ten cantos containing six hundred and forty-one stanzas. It opens with a description of the city of Kapilavastu (Kapilanagara). Then comes an account of Śuddhodana and his Queen Māyā. The second canto begins with an account of the visit of the gods to the Tuṣita Heaven. Next we find a description of the Tuṣita Heaven, which is followed by an

The Pitakaṭyalakkhaṇagandha.

The Padyacuḍāmaṇi.

Puggala Paññatti commentary, p. 254, "Visuddhi-Magge yaṁ vuttaṁ taṁ anādāya saṅkhatā...."

[1] The Padyacūḍāmaṇi of Buddhaghoṣācarya Edited by (the late) M. Ranga Achārya M.A., Rao Bahadur and by S. Kuppuswāmi Śāstrī, M.A., with a commentary by Paṇḍits K. Venkatesvara Śāstrī and D. S. Satakopa Ācharya. Published under the orders of the Government of Madras.

account of the gods' interview with the Lord of the place, and a description of the Lord in twenty-three verses. Then the gods uttered seventeen stanzas in praise of the Lord who being pleased with them, complied with their request to be born on earth as the son of Śuddhodana. The gods being delighted, went to their respective places and the Lord of the Tuṣita entered the womb of Māyā. The third canto opens with a description of Māyādevī in her state of pregnancy. In the tenth verse of the same canto, the birth of the child is described, followed by a long narrative of the incidents at his birth. Then comes an account of Śuddhodana's gifts at the birth of his son and the performance of the rites at child-birth and the naming of the child. Verses 33–41 contain an account of the prince's boyish sports. Then comes the account of his initiation and study, his attainment of youth and installation as heir-apparent. The fourth canto opens with a talk of marriage of the prince, the offer of a daughter by a Koliya chief and Śuddhodana's assent to it. Verses 4–35 contain an account of the decoration of the Koliya capital of the Koliya princess and of the princely bridegroom. Verses 36–53 describe the marriage ceremony, and the rest of the canto is devoted to an account of the prince's coming to Kapilavastu, the excitement of the women of Kapilavastu at his sight, etc. The fifth canto describes the enjoyments of the prince in the different seasons. King Śuddhodana then asked the prince to show him his skill in the use of weapons, which the latter promised to do on the seventh day. The canto closes with an account of the display of skill in the use of weapons by the prince. The sixth canto opens with a description of the spring. The prince goes out for sports in a garden. There the gods present before him, an old man, a sick man and a dead man. Next follow the prince's enquiry about them from his charioteers and their reply, his return to the city and his meeting with an ascetic, his questions to the charioteers about the ascetic and their reply. The canto ends with a description of the prince's desire to sport in the garden again. The seventh canto opens with a description of the garden. The prince goes to the lake for sporting in water. A description of the lake and sports occurs therein. The eighth canto gives a vivid picture of the sunset, and the darkness after sunset and contains a description of the sky and moonrise. The prince is next mentioned as entering his palace. The ninth canto opens with the prince seated on a beautiful couch and going through the ārātrika ceremony. Then comes a description of dancing, etc., in his presence. But he does not find any enjoyment in them and becomes moody. Then comes an account of the gods coming down and honouring him in various ways. Mention is then made, somewhat abruptly, of the prince's arrival after a journey of thirty yojanas to the Anovamā river (Pāli, Anomā). This is followed by a description of the river. The prince crosses the stream, sends away his followers, puts on the robe of a monk and practises penance. He dwells for some time by the side of the river Anovamā and goes to Rājagṛiha, the capital of Bimbisāra for alms.[1]

---

[1] The editors of the work as well as the commentators have referred to a Bimbasārapuri in verse 35. Bimbasārapuri is evidently a wrong reading for Bimbisārapuri or the city of King Bimbisāra, i.e. Rājagṛiha.

After going round the streets and collecting alms, he goes to the mountain called Pāṇḍava. There he takes his meal, enters a forest and practises austere penances for a long time. Not being able to attain Nirvāṇa by means of those austerities, he began to ponder the means of attaining his desired object. One night he dreamt five dreams. He awoke and understanding their meaning, ascertained that he would, on that very day, attain Nirvāṇa. Having performed his morning duties and waiting for the time of begging, he sat at the foot of a banyan tree. Then a woman brought a quantity of milk-rice for the deity residing in that tree. Taking him for the deity, she offered the pāyasa to him, and he too taking it, went to the side of the river Nerañjarā. There having bathed, he ate the food and spent the day in a sāla forest. Then towards the end of the day, he went to the Bodhi tree and scattered at its foot the Kusa grass brought by Brahmā. Then there appeared a great seat. He sat on it and the gods came and began to praise him. The canto closes with the mention of the appearance of Māra to overcome the Buddha. The tenth canto contains an account of the battle with Māra and his defeat by the Enlightened One.

An examination of the story of the life of the Buddha as given in the Padyacūḍāmaṇi shows that the author, in many places, differs from the generally accepted version derived from the Buddhist literature. The story of the gods' visit to the Tuṣita Heaven and their requesting the Bodhisatta to be born amongst men as described in the Padyacūḍāmaṇi canto II is found in the Dhammapada-aṭṭhakathā, Vol. I, p.

84 and in the Jātaka commentary, Vol. I, p. 48. But it is not given either in the Lalitavistara or in the Buddhacarita. It is now accepted on all hands that the Buddha was born in the Lummini garden. An Asokan pillar with an inscription still in situ verifies this fact. But no mention of the place of birth has been made in the Padyacūḍāmaṇi. The generally accepted tradition amongst the Buddhists is that the Buddha's mother, Queen Māyā, died soon after her child's birth. This fact, too, has been ignored in the work under review. The account in the sixth canto of the prince's going out for sports in the garden and seeing on the way an old man, a sick man and a dead man and his enquiry about them from the charioteers, differs from that given in the Mahāpadāna Sutta of the Dīgha Nikāya and in the Jātaka.[1] According to the story in the Jātaka commentary, the prince was driving in a chariot and when the omens appeared, he and the charioteer and none else saw them; and he put questions to the charioteer; but in the Padyacūḍāmaṇi mention has been made of more than one charioteer. According to the Pali Canon, Rāhula was born before the great retirement of Siddhārtha. The Buddhacarita also mentions the birth of Rāhula but the Padyacūḍāmaṇi is silent about it. The account of the retirement of Prince Siddhārtha as given in the ninth canto of the Padyacūḍāmaṇi is somewhat abrupt. The prince returns after sporting in the lake in the garden and on his return there were dancing, singing, etc. But he became averse to them and reached the banks of the

1 Fausboll, Vol. I, p. 59.

river Anovamā. According to the story in the Pāli Canon, Siddhārtha had, before his retirement, a look at his wife and Rāhula: and riding on Kanthaka accompanied by Channa, he left the palace. In the Padyacūḍāmaṇi (ninth canto), there is an account of his going to the city of Bimbisāra but no mention has been made of his meeting with that king. Verse 54 of the same canto mentions his practising austere penances but no mention has been made of his staying with Āḷāra Kālāma and Uddakarāmaputta. Verses 59 and 60 refer to the gift of pāyasa but the name of Sujātā has not been given. Verse 70 says that the Bodhisatta received from Brahmā the grass with which he prepared his seat. But the Pāli Canon records that the grass was given by Sotthiya, a grass-cutter. The work is concluded with the defeat of Māra by the Buddha—an incident with which the thirteenth canto of Aśwaghosa's Buddhacarita also ends. It is well-known that out of the seventeen cantos of the Buddhacarita, the first thirteen only are original and the last four were written by a scribe named Amritānanda.

The above detailed examination throws some doubt on the commentator Buddhaghosa's authorship of the Padyacūḍāmaṇi. Buddhaghosa was well acquainted with the traditions about the life of the Śākya Sage and it is quite unlikely that he should have omitted some of the important incidents of the life of the Great Teacher. The fact that the Padyacūḍāmaṇi ends exactly where the extant original portion of the Buddhacarita of Aśwaghoṣa comes to an end, is insignificant. The Buddhacarita was translated into Chinese in A.D. 420, i.e. very near to the time when Buddhaghosa flourished. It is very likely that Buddhaghosa saw the complete work of his illustrious predecessor, Aśwaghoṣa. The work under review was in all probability written by a man of inferior genius after the later cantos of the Buddha-carita had been lost. It might be that this work was written by Buddhaghosa who came later than the great commentator of the Pāli Buddhist Literature.

One other point requires consideration. The great commentator possessed, no doubt, a wide knowledge of Sanskrit literature, but there is no indication anywhere, in the accounts of his life as given in the Mahāvaṁsa or the later works like the Sāsanavaṁsa, etc., that he attempted to write anything in Sanskrit. He was devoted to the Pāli literature of which he was a past master, and it is not probable that he would go out of his way to compose a long poetical work in Sanskrit.

Other works of Buddhaghosa.

Turnour's Mahāvaṁsa and the Mahāyāzawin state that during his residence in Ceylon, Buddhaghosa translated into Pāli, the whole of the Sinhalese commentaries on the Tripiṭaka originally composed by Mahinda, the reputed son of the Emperor Aśoka and the Buddhist apostle of Ceylon. A Sinhalese compendium, on the other hand, states that he composed the Tripiṭaka, meaning probably his commentaries upon it, in Burma after his return from Ceylon. The Siamese legend respecting this portion of his work is somewhat confused.[1]

Spence Hardy mentions a commentary on the Buddha-

[1] Indian Antiquary, April, 1890, Vol. XIX, p. 118.

vaṁsa by him. This is probably the Aṭṭhakathā called the Maduratthavilāsinī whose authorship is assigned by Grimbolt not to Buddhaghosa but to a Buddhist monk living at the mouth of the Kāverī in Southern India.[1]

Buddhaghosa's works—a mine of historic interest.

A critical survey of Buddhaghosa's works suggests to the inquisitive student, many far reaching questions of which very few have indeed been hitherto examined or answered. His life, his social, religious and philosophical views, his reminiscences of Ceylon, his relations with Buddhadatta, his special contributions to the Buddhist thought, etc., all these can be gathered from his works. Buddhaghosa's works reveal the development of his own mind and are explanatory of his earlier thoughts. They bear testimony to his profound knowledge and vast erudition. About the value of Buddhaghosa's works Mrs. Rhys Davids observes, "It may readily be granted that Buddhaghosa must not be accepted *en bloc*. The distance between the constructive genius of Gotama and his apostles as compared with the succeeding ages of epigoni needs no depreciatory criticism on the labours of the exegetists to make itself felt forcibly enough. Buddhaghosa's philology is doubtless crude and he is apt to leave the cruces unexplained, concerning which an occidental is most in the dark. Nevertheless, to me his work is not only highly suggestive, but also a mine of historic interest. To put it aside is to lose the historical perspective of the course of the Buddhist Philosophy."[2]

---

[1] Indian Antiquary, April, 1890, Vol. XIX, p. 119.

[2] Mrs. Rhys Davids, A Buddhist Manual of Psychological Ethics, Introductory Essay, p. xxv.

R. C. Childers rightly speaks of him thus: "Buddhaghosa did not confine himself to translate Mahendra, but incorporated other old Sinhalese chronicles existing in his time, and added immense contributions, chiefly exegetical, of his own. Much of the matter his commentaries contain, is as old as the Tripiṭaka itself, while, like the Tripiṭaka, they are rich in history and folk-lore and abound in narratives which shed a flood of light on the social and moral condition of Ancient India." A rich legacy has been left by him to the Buddhist Literature. Gray in his introduction to the Buddhaghosuppatti records thus: "Suvaṇṇabhūmi in particular has good reason to be proud of him. Siam derived the Buddhist scriptures from her, as is clear from Talaing chronicles, and the debt of gratitude which Burma owed to Ceylon was sufficiently repaid when, after the total destruction of Buddhistic literature by the Malabars in the twelfth century, she was able to return to that sacred island a copy of the very books she had borrowed seven centuries before and preserved with most zealous care." (pp. 31 32). Gray further records, "Buddhaghosa's commentaries as they now exist in Ceylon, were taken over from Pagan in Burma. No copy of them could have been kept by the Sinhalese priests after he first compiled them, otherwise Fa-Hien, who visited Anurādhapura after Buddhaghosa, would most certainly have mentioned them and taken at least a copy of the commentary on the Vinaya." (p. 32)

Thanks are due to the labours of the late Professor T. W. Rhys Davids and Mrs. Rhys Davids, the founders of the Pāli Text Society, Surrey and its other workers for publishing some of the important works of Buddhaghosa, namely the Visuddhimagga, portions of the Sumaṅgalavilāsinī, the Atthasālinī, the Puggala Paññatti commentary, the Dhammapada commentary, the Kathāvatthu commentary, and the Paṭṭhāna commentary. We are glad to find that they have undertaken to print a few other books of the great commentator, namely, the Manorathapūraṇī, the Sammohavinodanī, the Sāratthapakāsinī, the Samantapāsādikā and the remaining portions of the Sumaṅgalavilāsinī. These, no doubt, are and will be the permanent works of the society and from them the world will know more about Buddhism.

CHAPTER V

THE SUCCESSORS OF BUDDHAGHOSA

Buddhaghosa's work left unfinished.

Buddhaghosa is credited by the Mahāvaṁsa with having written commentaries on the whole of the Buddhist Tripiṭaka. But, as we have seen in the last chapter, though he wrote commentaries on a very large portion of all the three piṭakas, yet a considerable portion remained unattempted by him. Perhaps he found his life too short for the completion of the huge work to which he devoted his life, or perhaps he found his health failing; or, if we are to believe that he did actually return to India, other causes which we cannot conjecture might have intervened before he could finish the remaining books of the Holy Canon.

But completed by his successors.

The work thus left unfinished was taken up by others who came after him and it will be interesting here to give an account of persons who, following in the footsteps of the great commentator, served to make Buddhist literature easily intelligible to succeeding generations.

Among these successors of Buddhaghosa the following are noteworthy[1] :—

1. Buddhadatta, the reputed author of—

   Uttaravinicchayo.

---

[1] J.P.T.S., 1886, pp. 59–63.

Vinayavinicchayo.
Adhidhammāvatāra.
Madhuratthavilāsinī, a commentary on the Buddhavaṁsa.

2. Dhammapālācariyo who wrote—
Nettipakaraṇa-aṭṭhakathā.
Itivuttaka-aṭṭhakathā.
Udāna-aṭṭhakathā.
Cariyāpiṭaka-aṭṭhakathā.
Theragāthā-aṭṭhakathā.
Vimalavilāsinī, a commentary on the Vimānavatthu.
Vimalavilāsinī, a commentary on the Petavatthu.
Paramatthamañjūsā.
Līnatthapakāsinī.
Paramatthadīpanī.
Līnatthavaṇṇanā, etc.

3. Mahānāma who wrote the Saddhammapakāsinī, a commentary on the Paṭisaṁbhidāmagga.
4. Moggallāna (navo), author of the Abhidhānappadīpikā.
5. Cullabuddhaghosa, author of the Jātattagīnidānaṁ and Sotattagīnidānaṁ.

Buddhaghosa and Buddhadatta.

Buddhadatta, the first of these commentators, is supposed to have been a contemporary of Buddhaghosa. According to the account given in the Buddhaghosuppatti, Buddhaghosa is said to have sailed for Ceylon after taking his preceptor's permission the very day that Buddhadatta left Ceylon for Jambudvīpa. He was in the ship for three days. Through the supernatural powers of Sakka, the ships of the two theras came in contact with each other. The merchants who were on the vessel of Buddhadatta saw Buddhaghosa and were frightened. Buddhaghosa came out and seeing the merchants frightened, asked, "Who is the monk in your ship"? The merchants replied, "Buddhadatta." Buddhadatta then came out and saw the thera and asked his name. Buddhaghosa replied, "I am Buddhaghosa." Buddhadatta asked, "Where are you going"? Buddhaghosa replied, "I am going to Ceylon." Buddhadatta asked, "What for"? He replied, "The teaching of the Lord is written in Ceylonese and I am going to render it into Māgadhi." Buddhadatta said, "I have written Jīnālaṅkāra, Dantadhātubodhivaṁsa and not the aṭṭhakathās and the ṭīkās; if you render the teaching of the Lord into Māgadhi from Sinhalese, you write out the aṭṭhakathās of the three piṭakas." Thus Buddhadatta gave some task to Buddhaghosa to perform. He also gave him myrobalan, the iron style and a stone, and added, "If you have eye disease or pain in the back, you rub this myrobalan on the stone and apply, surely your pain will disappear." Buddhaghosa on his part praised the Jīnālaṅkāra of Buddhadatta and said, "Your book is very deep, it is difficult for the unwise to understand it." Buddhadatta in his turn exhorted Buddhaghosa thus, "I came to the island of Ceylon before you to write out the teaching of the Lord into Māgadhi from Sinhalese. I am short-lived, I won't live long, you perform the task." As soon as the conversation ended, the vessels became separated,[1] Buddhaghosa sailed for Ceylon and Buddhadatta for Jambudvīpa.

The known facts about Buddhadatta may be told in a few words. The thera[2] was a celebrity of the Mahāvihāra of Ceylon, and was an inhabitant of the Cola Kingdom situated on the Kāverī. He tells us that his royal patron was King Accutavikkanta of the Kalamba dynasty. All his works were written in the famous monastery erected by Veṇhudāsa or Kaṇhadāsa on the banks of the Kāverī.[3]

The Rev. A. P. Buddhadatta has prepared an edition of his notable namesake's Abhidhammāvatāra, i.e. an 'introduction to philosophy.' Buddhaghosa expounds his psychology in terms of the five khandhas. Buddhadatta opens his scheme with a fourfold division of the compendium, viz. mind, mental properties, material quality and nibbāṇa. In this respect Buddhadatta's representation is perhaps better than that of Buddhaghosa.[4]

---

[1] Buddhaghosuppatti, edited by J. Gray, pp. 49–51. The same account also occurs in the Sāsanavaṁsa (edited by M. Bode), pp. 29 and 30. "Evaṁ tesaṁ dvinnaṁ therānaṁ aññamaññaṁ sallapantānaṁ yeva dve nāvā sayaṁ eva apanetvā gacchiṁsu.

[2] According to the Gandhavaṁsa, Buddhadatta came next to Buddhaghosa. J.P.T.S., 1886, p. 59.

[3] Abhidhammāvatāra, P.T.S., Viññāpanaṁ, xiii, xiv, xv, xvi, and xvii.

"....Vinayavinicchayo....
....Coḷaraṭṭhe Bhūtamaṅgala-gāme
Veṇhudāsassa ārāme vasantena
Accutavikkama-nāmassa coḷarañño kāle kato."
"Kāverī-paṭṭane ramme, nānārāmopasobhite
Kārite Kaṇhadāsena dassanīye manorame."
(Abhidhammāvatāra.)

"....Buddhadattenaracito'yan Vinaya-Vinicchayo."
(Vinaya-Vinicchaya.)

[4] Mrs. Rhys Davids, Buddhist Psychology (Quest Series), p. 174.

There is no reason to disbelieve the statement that the two teachers met each other. It is clear that they drew materials from the same source. This fact well explains why the Visuddhimagga and the Abhidhammāvatāra have so many points in common. Buddhadatta has rendered great service to the study of the Abhidhamma tradition which has survived in Theravāda Buddhism to the present day. The legendary account is that Buddhadatta put in a condensed shape that which Buddhaghosa handed on in Pāli from the Sinhalese commentaries. " But the psychology and philosophy are presented through the prism of a second vigorous intellect, under the fresh aspects in a style often less discursive and more graphic than that of the great commentator, and with a strikingly rich vocabulary."

It is also narrated in the account we have referred to above that when on sea Buddhadatta met Buddhaghosa and learnt that he was going to Ceylon to render the Sinhalese commentaries into Pāli, he spoke to the latter thus, " When you finish the commentaries, please send them to me, so that I may summarise your labours." Buddhaghosa said that he would comply with his request and the narrative adds that the Pāli commentaries were after completion actually placed in the hands of Buddhadatta who summed up the commentaries on the Abhidhamma in the Abhidhammāvatāra and those on the Vinaya in the Vinayavinicchaya (abridged translation of the foregoing by the editor, Buddhadatta's Manual, p. xix). Mrs. Rhys Davids says, " It is probably right to conclude that they both were but handing on an analytical formula, which had evolved between their own time and that of the final closing of the Abhidhamma Piṭaka." [1]

Like Buddhaghosa, Buddhadatta, too, employed the simile of the purblind and the lame to explain the relation between Nāma and Rūpa.[2] Buddhadatta's division of the terms into Samūha and Asamūha is another interesting point.[3] It will be remembered that such a division of terms as this was far in advance of the older classification embodied in the Puggala Paññatti commentary.[4]

Supposing that Kumāra Gupta I of the Imperial Gupta dynasty was a contemporary of King Mahānāma of Ceylon and that Buddhaghosa was a contemporary of Thera Buddhadatta, it follows that King Accutavikkanta of Kalamba dynasty was a contemporary of Kumāra Gupta I.

According to Rev. A. P. Buddhadatta,[5] Buddhadatta was either older than Buddhaghosa or of the same age with him. This statement is, however, doubtful. In the Buddhaghosuppatti[6] we find Buddhadatta addressed Buddhaghosa by the epithet 'āvuso,' which is applied to one who is

---

1 Mrs. Rhys Davids, Buddhist Psychology (Quest Series), p. 179.

2 Abhidhammāvatāra, P.T.S., p. 115.

"Namaṁ nissāya rūpan tu, rūpaṁ nissāya nāmakaṁ
pavattati sadā sabbaṁ, pañcavokāra-bhūmiyaṁ;
imassa pana atthassa, āvibhāvatthaṁ eva ca
jaccandha-pīṭhasappīnaṁ, vattabbā upamā idha."

3 Abhidhammāvatāra, P.T.S , p. 83.

"Upādā-paññatti nāma samūhāsamūha-vasena duvidhā hoti."

4 Cf. Puggala-Paññatti commentary, P.T.S., p. 173.

5 Buddhadatta's Manual edited by Rev. A. P. Buddhadatta, pp. xiii and xiv. "Ayaṁ pana Buddhadattācariyo Buddhaghosācariyena samāna-vassiko vā thokaṁ vuḍḍhataro vā ti sallakkhema."

6 p. 50.

younger in age. The passage runs thus, "Āvuso Buddhaghosa, ahaṁ tayā pubbe Laṅkādīpe Bhagavato sāsanam kātum āgatomhī ti vatvā aham appāyuko....." This shows that according to the tradition recorded in the Buddhaghosuppatti, Buddhaghosa was younger than Buddhadatta.

The different accounts of the comparative age of Buddhadatta and Buddhaghosa are hardly reconciliable. The account given in the Introduction to the Abhidhammāvatāra clearly shows that Buddhadatta lived to write abridgements of some of Buddhaghosa's works. This goes against the legend contained in the Buddhaghosuppatti that Buddhadatta left Ceylon earlier than Buddhaghosa without translating the Ceylonese Aṭṭhakathā, apprehending that he was not to live long.

Buddhaghosa and Dhammapāla.

The Sāsanavaṁsa records that ācariya Dhammapālathero dwelt at Padaratittha in the Kingdom of Damiḷa near Ceylon. It is for this reason that he should be regarded as one of the Sinhalese commentators ("So ca ācariya-Dhammapālathero Sīhaladīpassa samīpe Damiḷaraṭṭhe Padaratitthaṁhi nivāsitattā Sīhaḷadīpe yeva samgahetvā vattabbo." [1]) He also must have based his commentary on the Sinhalese Aṭṭhakathās, as these were not preserved on the mainland, as we have seen from the accounts we have already given.

T. W. Rhys Davids is of the opinion that Buddhaghosa

[1] Sāsanavaṁsa, p. 33.

and Dhammapāla seem to have been educated at the same University. In support of this view he refers to the published works of the two writers, a careful study of which shows that they hold very similar views, they appeal to the same authorities, they have the same method of exegesis, they have reached the same stage in philological and etymological science and they have the same lack of any knowledge of the simplest rules of the higher criticism. The conclusion follows that as far as we can at present judge, they must have been trained in the same school. (Hasting's Encyclopædia of Religion and Ethics, Vol. 4, p. 701.)

Mrs. Rhys Davids says in her introduction to the translation of the Therī-gāthā, "in the fifth or sixth century A.D., either before or just after Buddhaghosa had flourished, and written his great commentaries on the prose works of the Vinaya and Sutta Piṭakas, Dhammapāla of Kāñcipura (now Conjevaram), wrote down in Pāli the unwritten expository material constituting the then extant three Aṭṭhakathās on the Psalms and incorporated it into his commentary on the three other books of the Canon, naming the whole 'Paramatthadīpanī' or *Elucidation of the Ultimate Meaning*. He not only gives the *ākhyāna* in each Psalm, but adds a paraphrase in the Pāli of his day, of the more archaic idiom in which the *gāthās* were compiled."[1]

From the commentaries of Dhammapāla, it appears that he was well-read and well-informed. His explanation of terms is very clear. His commentaries throw consider-

[1] Mrs. Rhys Davids, Psalms of the Sisters, p. xvi.

able light on the social, religious, moral and philosophical ideas of the time like the commentaries of Buddhaghosa. He was not only the author of the Paramatthadīpanī but also of several other works[1] such as the Petavatthuaṭṭhakathā. In short, his works remind us of the commentaries of Buddhaghosa.

Mrs. Rhys Davids says, "the presentation of verses, solemn or otherwise, in a framework of prose narrative is essentially the historical Buddhist way of imparting canonical poetry. Dhammapāla's chronicles are, for the most part, unduplicated in any other extant work; but not seldom they run on all fours, not only with parallel chronicles in Buddhaghosa's commentaries, but also with the prose framework of poems in Sutta-Nipāta or Samyutta Nikāya, not to mention the Jātaka." We quite agree with Mrs. Rhys Davids on this point (Mrs. Rhys Davids' Psalms of the Brethren, p. xxv).

[1] Gandhavaṁsa, p. 60, cf. Sāsanavaṁsa, p. 33.

CHAPTER VI

THE ENCYCLOPÆDIC CHARACTER OF BUDDHAGHOSA'S WORKS

Buddhaghosa was not merely a metaphysician. His scholarship was wide and deep. His information was vast. His works abound in references to History, Geography, Astronomy, Dancing, Music, Anatomy, Bird-life, Jugglery and so forth. He had a fair knowledge of the vegetable kingdom.

Astronomy.

Buddhaghosa was not ignorant of astronomy. His astronomical knowledge is evidenced by his reference to the measurement of the size of Rāhu, the Dragon.[1]

Grammar.

It is stated in the Visuddhimagga that Buddhaghosa was a great grammarian, and a great poet, and also was well-versed in analytical knowledge. It appears that he studied the great grammar of Pāṇini. In the Visuddhimagga (P.T.S. Edition, pp. 491–492, 'Indriyasaccaniddeso') we read:—

"Ko pana nesaṁ indriyaṭṭho nāmāti? Indaliṅgaṭṭho indriyaṭṭho; indadesitaṭṭho indriyaṭṭho; indadiṭṭhaṭṭho indriyaṭṭho; indasiṭṭhaṭṭho indriyaṭṭho; indajuṭṭhaṭṭho indriyaṭṭho: so sabbo pi idha yathāyogam yujjati. Bhagavā hi sammāsaṁbuddho paramissariyabhāvato indo, kusalākusalañ ca kammaṁ, kammesu kassaci issariyābhāvato. Ten'ev'ettha

[1] Kindred Sayings, p. 72.

kammasañjanitāni tāva indriyāni kusalākusalakammaṁ ullingenti. Tena ca siṭṭhānīti indalingaṭṭhena indasiṭṭhaṭṭhena ca indriyāni. Sabbān'eva pan'etāni Bhagavatā yathābhūtato pakāsitāni abhisaṁbuddhāni cā ti indadesitaṭṭhena indadiṭṭhaṭṭhena ca indriyāni. Ten'eva Bhagavatā munindena kānici gocarāsevanāya, kānici bhāvanāsevanāya sevitānīti indajuṭṭhaṭṭhenāpi etāni indriyāni."

Buddhaghosa goes on to add :—

'Api ca ādhipaccasaṅkhātena issariyaṭṭhenā pi etāni indriyāni. Cakkhuviññāṇādippavattiyaṁ hi cakkhādīnaṁ siddham ādhipaccaṁ, tasmim tikkhe tikkhattā, mande mandattāti. Ayaṁ tāv' ettha atthato vinicchayo.'

These explanations of '*Indriya*' are evidently a reminiscence of Pāṇini, V. 2, 93. "Indriyaṁ indraliṅgaṁ indradṛṣṭaṁ indrajuṣṭaṁ indradattaṁ iti vā."

In the grammar of Pāṇini, there is mention of *āpatti* in the sense of prāpti and in this sense too, *āpatti* occurs several times in the Samantapāsādikā. This seems also to show that Buddhaghosa knew of and utilised the work of Pāṇini.

His geographical information is not very meagre as is clear from the following :—

Geography.

He defines Dakshiṇāpatha or the Deccan as the tract of land lying to the south of the Ganges.[2] He records that the Godāvarī forms the border line between the territories of two Andhra Kings (Dvinnaṁ Andhakarājānaṁ), that is to say, between Assaka and Aḷaka.[3] In Buddha-

---

[1] J.P.T.S. 1906–07, pp. 172–173.

[2] Sumaṅgalavilāsinī, Vol. I, p. 265, "Dakkhiṇa-patho ti pākaṭaṁ Gaṅgāya dakkhiṇato pākaṭa-janapadaṁ."

[3] Paramatthajotikā, Sutta Nipāta Commentary, II, p. 581.

ghosa's time, Assaka and Aḷaka were the two Andhra Kings or rather kingdoms. His personal acquaintance with the Andhra countries is evident from his detailed account of an island in the middle of the Godāvarī.[1] The Ganges on the north and the Godāvarī on the south are uppermost in his mind.[2] Of the country below the Godāvarī, however, he does not appear to have possessed much knowledge.

Of Northern India, especially of North-eastern India which, according to tradition, was his birth-place, Buddhaghosa gives a little more information in his writings. In the Sumaṅgalavilāsinī, in connection with the city of Campā, the capital of Aṅga, he says that not far from the city, there was the tank Gaggarā, so called because it was dug by a Queen named Gaggarā. On its banks all around, there was a great forest of Campaka trees decorated with flowers of five colours, blue, etc.[3] This account of Campā has, however, hardly any geographical value. He also gives us his own interpretation of the term Aṅga. According to him, it is so called because of the beauty of the princes of the country.[4] The explanation seems to be rather fanciful. He mentions Magadha

[1] Sutta-Nipāta Commentary, p. 581.

[2] Atthasālinī (P.T.S.) p. 140. "Tato nikkhantattā pana akusalaṁ pi Gaṅgāya nikkhantā nadī Gaṅgā viya Godāvarīto nikkhantā Godāvarī viya ca paṇḍaram tveva vuttam."

[3] Sumaṅgalavilāsinī, pt. I, pp. 279–80— "Tassa Campā-nagarassa avidūre Gaggarāya nāma rāja-mahesiyā khāṇitattā Gaggarā ti laddha-vohārā pokkharaṇī atthi. Tassa tīre samantato nīlādi-pañca-vaṇṇa-kusuma-paṭimaṇḍitaṁ mahantaṁ campaka vanaṁ."

[4] Ibid, p. 279. "Aṅgā nāma aṅga-pāsādikatāya evaṁ laddha-vohārā jānapadino rāja-kumārā."

as a country of the princes known as Magadhas.[1] In his Sumaṅgalavilāsinī to the Mahāli Sutta in the Dīgha Nikāya, Buddhaghosa gives us an interesting account of the Mahāvana in the neighbourhood of Vaiśālī and of the double-galleried vihāra which stood in it. In commenting upon the word 'Mahāvana', he says, "Outside the town lying in one stretch up to the Himalayas, there is a natural forest which on account of the large area covered by it, is called 'Mahāvana.'"[2] Buddhaghosa also offers a comment explaining the origin of the name Kūṭāgārasālā. "In that forest was established a Saṅghārāma or monastery. A pāsāda or a storied building was built on pillars, a pinnacle was put above it and it was made into a Kūṭāgārasālā resembling a mansion of devas (devavimāna). From it, all Sangharamas or monasteries are known as Kūṭāgārasālās."[3] This agrees with the description given by Fā-Hien of the double-galleried Vihāra. Our commentator shows an intimate acquaintance with the city of Vesālī; and about its rulers, the Licchavis, he offers much valuable information.

Account of Indian Sects.

He had a fair knowledge of the history of the various sects of ascetics. He was acquainted with the opinions of the Ājivikas and the Niganṭhas, as appears from his obser-

---

[1] Sumaṅgalavilāsinī, p. 294. "Magadhā nāma jānapadino rāja-kumārā. Tesaṁ-nivāso eko pi janapado rūḷhisaddena Magadhā ti vuccati."

[2] Sumaṅgalavilāsinī, pt. I, p. 309, "Bahinagare Himavantena saddhiṁ ekābaddhaṁ hutvā ṭhitaṁ sayañ-jāta-vanaṁ atthi, yaṁ mahantabhāven'eva Mahavanaṁti vuccati."

[3] Ibid, p. 309. "Tasmiṁ vana-saṇḍe saṁghārāmaṁ patiṭṭhāpesuṁ. Tattha kaṇṇikaṁ yojetvā thambhānaṁ upari kūṭāgāra-sālā-saṁkhepena deva-vimāna-sadi-

vations regarding their views of the soul after death.[1] He gives us bits of the life-history of the teachers of the various sects mentioned in the Vinaya and the Nikāyas. He speaks of Pūraṇa Kassapa as one of the teachers who went about naked.[2] Pūraṇa was his name and Kassapa was his family or gotra name. He fled to a forest where his clothes were snatched away by robbers. In his nude state, he entered a village where he was held as a holy mendicant. (Sumaṅgala-vilāsinī, Vol. I, p. 142.)

Regarding Pakudha Kaccāyana, we are told that he did not use cold water. He used hot water or hot rice-gruel. (Sumaṅgalavilāsinī, p 144.)

As to Gosāla, Buddhaghosa says that, in his opinion, things happen exactly as they are to happen, that which is not to happen does not happen. (Sumaṅgalavilāsinī, pp. 160–5.) Makkhali was the personal name of this teacher and he was called Gosāla because he was born in a cow-pen. One day he was ordered to carry an oil-pot along a muddy slippery path. His master told him, "Tāta, mā khalīti." But his feet slipped on account of his carelessness; and for the fear of his master he began to flee. His master caught the end of his garment but he ran on naked leaving the garment behind. (Sumaṅgalavilāsinī, p. 144.)

With regard to Ajītakesakambalin, Buddhaghosa says that Ajīta was his proper name. His nickname was Kesa-kambalin (hair-blanket) because he used to wear a blanket

---

saṁ pāsādaṁ akaṁsu. Taṁ upādāya sakalo pi saṁghārāmo Kūṭāgāra-sālā ti paññāyittha."

[1] Dialogues of the Buddha, pt. 1, p. 44 f.n.   [2] Ibid., p. 69 f.n.

made of human hair. This blanket, according to Buddhaghosa, is the worst of all garments, being cold in winter and warm in summer and it is the cheapest and it is rough and ugly and emits a bad smell. (Sumaṅgalavilāsinī, p. 144).

Buddhaghosa tells us that after a Hall had been established in Queen Mallikā's park at Sāvatthī, others near it were built in honour of the various famous teachers but the group of buildings continued to be known as "the Hall." There the Brahmins, the Nigaṇṭhas, the Acelakas, the Paribbājakas and other teachers met and expounded or discussed their views.[1]

Buddhaghosa records in his Sumaṅgalavilāsinī (pp. 138–139) an account of Devadatta who requested the Buddha to give him the leadership of the Bhikkhusaṁgha but was refused. Again he came to the Buddha with the request to introduce some hard and fast monastic rules enacting that Bhikkhus must not take fish and flesh, they must put on three robes only and they must live under the open sky, always living on alms etc., but the Buddha did not comply with his request. This dissatisfied him and he got together some followers and made a Saṁgha separate from the Bhikkhusaṁgha of the Buddha. This Saṁgha of Devadatta flourished for some time. Shortly afterwards Devadatta lost his prestige. He succeeded in persuading Ajātaśatru to become his follower, by showing him a miracle. It was he who induced Ajātaśatru to torture his father Bimbisāra

[1] Dialogues of the Buddha, p. 244 f.n.

to death and to become the King of Magadha. He himself made several attempts to kill the Buddha but in vain. At last he wanted to see the Buddha but he was swallowed up by the earth by the side of a pond at Jetavana.

Account of Indian tribes.

Buddhaghosa further supplies us with important and interesting information regarding the Mallas, the Śākyas, the Koliyas, the Licchavis and so forth. He says that the Mallas were Kṣatriyas[1] forming an oligarchy of rājās.[2]

Regarding the Śākyas, he says that the great clan of Gotama's relations consisted of eighty thousand families on the father's side and the like number on the mother's side.[3] This number has, we think, hardly any historical value: it is evidently used to signify a very large number. In the Sumaṅgalavilāsinī, we have an account of the origin of the Śākyas and their matrimonial alliances with the Koliyas.[4] It is recorded that the Śākyas did not show respect to the Brahmins.[5] The Pāsādika Suttanta of the Digha Nikāya informs us that the Exalted One was once sojourning among the Śākyas at the technical college in the Mango-grove of the Śākya family. From the above, it is obvious that the Śākyas had a technical college of their own. Buddhaghosa supplies us with the information that it was a long terraced mansion made for the learning of crafts.[6]

1 Dialogues of the Buddha, pt. II, p. 141.

2 Ibid., pt. III, p. 201. 3 Ibid., pt. I, p. 147. 4 p. 258 foll.

5 Sumaṅgalavilāsinī, p. 256. "Ime Sakyā na brāhmaṇe sakkaronti."

6 Dialogues of the Buddha, pt. III, p. 111.

Regarding the Licchavis, also, the great commentator furnishes us with some interesting particulars. In his Paramatthajotikā on the Khuddakapāṭha, he splits the name 'Licchavi' into 'Līnā-chavi' = Licchavi = Nicchavi. He says that things in their stomach appeared to be attached to their 'chavi' or 'skin,' and hence they were called Licchavis.[1] According to him, there was a festival among the Licchavis called Sabbarattivāra or Sabbaratticara. In it, songs were sung, trumpets, drums and other musical instruments were used and flags were flown. Kings, princes and commanders-in-chief took part in the festival and spent the whole night in merry-making.[2] The women were not wholly excluded from convivial gatherings. It is stated in the Dhammapadaṭṭhakathā that the Licchavis used to go to gardens with the beauties of the town (nagarasobhinī).

In the Sumaṅgalavilāsinī,[4] we read that there was a port near the Ganges and a mountain not far from it, and that at the foot of the mountain there was a mine of precious gems. Some precious gems were washed away by the Ganges, and there was a contract between the Licchavis and King Ajātaśatru of Magadha that they would divide the gems equally. But the avaricious Licchavis did not fulfil the agreement. This enraged Ajātaśatru very much. He thought of punishing them for this act. He

[1] P.T.S., p. 159, " Sibbetvā ṭhapitā viya nesaṁ aññamaññaṁ līnā chavi ahosi."

[2] Dhammapada-aṭṭhakathā, Vol. III, p. 460.

[3] P.T.S , Vol. III, pp. 279–280.

[4] Sumaṅgalavilāsinī, (Burmese edition, Simon Hewavitarne's Bequest Series, No 1. Revised by Ñānissara, p. 99.)

realized, however, that the Licchavis being numerically stronger, he would fail to carry out his purpose. He tried to be friendly with the Licchavis, but he had to give up this idea. At last he resorted to the device of sowing dissensions and he was successful. Through his machinations the unity of the Licchavis was almost broken, with the result that the poor among the Licchavis began to hate the rich, and the strong looked down upon the weak. At that psychological moment, Ajātaśatru took advantage of the internal dissensions amongst the Licchavis and invaded the Vajjian territory. The weaker Licchavis refused to stand against him and said, "Let the strong Licchavis go forward and crush him." Thus it was easy for Ajātaśatru to conquer Vesālī, the capital of the Vajjians.

Buddhaghosa also gives other interesting particulars about the Licchavis. If a Licchavi fell ill, the other Licchavis came to see him. Chastity was not to be violated by force. The old religious rites were observed. The whole clan would join any auspicious ceremony performed in the house of a Licchavi. When a foreign king paid a visit to the Licchavi country, the Licchavis went out in a body to receive him and to do him honour. They sent out armies at the approach of foreign invaders. With regard to the financial administration of the Licchavis, Buddhaghosa tells us that they were averse to the imposition of new taxes. Old taxes were kept up. The Vajjians used to learn Rājanīti or the science of state-craft from their old experienced countrymen. They used to hold frequent meetings at which matters relating to various parts of the country were heard and discussed. By beat of drum the meeting was announced and every one tried to attend and the work being done, they all dispersed at the same time.[1] Besides political matters, subjects of general interest, such as questions of religion, were discussed at these meetings of the Licchavis.

It is stated in the Sumaṅgalavilāsinī that Sīha, a novice, saw a large assembly of the Licchavis and thought thus, "Surely the Blessed One will most gladly preach Dhamma in this assembly."[2] In the Samantapāsādikā, Buddhaghosa states that this assembly was like the assembly of the Tāvatiṁsa devas.[3]

In his Sumaṇgalavilāsinī, the commentator records a saying of Mahāli, a Licchavi: "I am a Kṣatriya, so is the Buddha; if his knowledge increases and he becomes all-knowing, why should it not happen to me."[4] In the same work, we have a picture of the administration of justice among the Licchavis. When a thief is caught, he is brought before the judge who can acquit him if he thinks him not guilty, but if he thinks him guilty, he cannot inflict punishment upon him, but he can send him to the *Vohārika* who, if he thinks punishment necessary, sends him to the *Antokāriko* who, in his turn, can send him to the *Senāpati*; if he is convinced of his guilt, he can send him to the *Uparājā* who, again, if he thinks him guilty, sends him to the *Rājā*; the *Rājā*, as the highest court of appeal, could inflict punish-

1 Sumaṅgalavilāsinī (Burmese edition), pp. 103–105. 2 p. 310.
3 Samantapāsādikā (Burmese edition), p. 338.
4 Sumaṅgalavilāsinī, pt. I, p. 312.

ment upon him according to the Paveṇipotthaka, i.e. Book of Precedents.[1]

Account of Indian kings and nobles.

Buddhaghosa gives us a history of Bimbisāra, king of Magadha. According to him, the king was the lord of the Magadhese. He is called 'Seṇiya', as he was associated with a large army. He was called Bimbisāra, because his body was like gold ('Bimbi' means golden). He further records that Ajātaśatru, son of Bimbisāra, was the issue of Vaidehī,[2] the daughter of the king of Kośala.[3]

The Papañcasūdanī[4] names Mahārāja Mahākośala as a king of Kośala. Bimbisāra was the contemporary king of Magadha. The king of Kośala gave his own daughter, Vai-

---

[1] Porāṇaṁ Vajjidhammanti-ettha pubbe kira Vajjirājāno ayaṁ 'coro' ti ānetva dassite, gaṇhatha taṁ coran ti avatvā vinicchayamahāmattānaṁ denti. Te pi vinicchinitvā sace acoro hoti, vissajjenti, sace coro hoti, attano kiñci avatvā Vohārikānaṁ denti, tepi vinicchinitvā acoro ce vissajjenti, coro ce Suttadharā (different reading, Antokārikā-Burmese manuscript) nāma honti, tesam denti; te pi vinicchinitvâ acoro ce vissajjenti, coro ce Aṭṭhakulikānaṁ denti, te pi tath'eva katvā Senāpatissa, Senāpati Uparājassa, Uparājā Rañño, rājā vinicchinitvā acoro ce vissajjenti; sace panacoro hoti, "Paveṇipotthakaṁ" vācāpeti, tattha "yena idaṁ nāma katam, tassa ayaṁ nāma daṇḍo ti likhitaṁ" rājā tassa kiriyam tena samānetvā tadanucchavikaṁ daṇḍam karotīti eva porāṇam Vajjidhammaṁ. Sumaṅgalavilāsinī edited by Dhammakitti Siri Devamitta Mahāthera, Vol. I, p. 356. (Simon Hewavitarṇe Bequest Series, Colombo.)

[2] Dialogues of the Buddha, Pt. I, p. 65.

[3] Rhys Davids in his Buddhist India, p. 3, speaks of Ajātaśatru as the son of Bimbisāra by a Videha lady from Mithilā. But Buddhaghosa in his Sumaṇgalavilāsinī, pt. I, p. 139, distinctly says that he was the son of the daughter of the king of Kośala and not of the king of Videha. The princess was called Vaidehī because of her scholarship ("Vedehi—putto ti ayaṁ Kosalarañño dhītāya putto, na Videha-rañño. Vedehīti pana paṇḍitādhivacanaṁ etaṁ").

[4] MSS. of this work kindly lent to me by Revd. A. Dhammapāla.

dehī, in marriage to Bimbisāra. After the death of Mahākośala, Pasenadī ascended the throne of Kośala. Sāvatthī was his capital. When the Buddha went to Rājagaha, Bimbisāra with his family became his follower.

In his commentary on the Majjhima-Nikāya, Buddhaghosa gives the following detailed account of king Pasenadī who was the ruler of Kośala at the time the Buddha preached his religion. Buddhaghosa must have derived his information from the Aṭṭhakathās or other authentic records, so here may be some bits of genuine historical information.

The fame of the Buddha spread far and wide and it reached Pasenadī who was envious of the great teacher. At first he sided with the heretics against the Buddha. It was at his instigation that some heretics spread a false report. They showed the dead body of a beautiful girl, and said that Gotama, in order to hide his sins, concealed the dead body under a heap of dried flowers near the Gandhakuṭi, but the fraud was soon detected and the Buddha's fame increased greatly. Pasenadī and the Buddha were of the same age. He loved the Brahmins very much and gave them large tracts of land.

In order to put a stop to the misdeeds of the heretics, the Buddha sent Sāriputta to king Pasenadī who at first refused to see him. Afterwards he became a convert and did immense service to the Buddhist Saṁgha. The female members of his family were engaged in doing service to the Buddha. His own wife Mallikā devoted herself to the lifelong service of the True Law. The Kośalan monarch's faith in the Buddha became so strong that he sought the aid of the Buddha in great and small affairs.[1]

Mahākośala had given a large village[2] to meet the expenses of Vaidehī. Pasenadī being dissatisfied with Ajātaśatru, son of Vaidehī, because he had ascended the throne of Magadha after killing his father, took that village from him by force and a great war ensued between uncle and nephew. Pasenadī was repeatedly defeated but he at last defeated Ajātaśatru and took him prisoner.

During the reign of Pasenadī, Kośala was very much troubled by Aṅgulimāla, the great bandit. Many people left the country. The king went out with five hundred cavalries to capture the robber. He first went to Jetavana Vihāra to see the Buddha once. The Blessed One saw the army and asked why the king had come with such a force. He added that he alone would bring the robber round. At that time Aṅgulimāla was with the Buddha and the latter introduced him thus, "O, Mahārāja, this is Aṅgulimāla." On hearing this, the king was terrified.[3]

Pasenadī used to visit the Buddha often and listened to religious instructions. In the Saṁyutta Nikāya, we have a chapter called 'Kosala-Saṁyutta,' especially devoted to the religious discourse between Pasenadī and the Buddha. In his commentary on this topic Buddhaghosa recounts the following narrative :—

Pasenadī first met the Buddha at Jetavana. He asked

---

[1] Cf. Kosala-Saṁyutta, Saṁyutta N. (P.T.S.), Book III, pt. I, pp. 68 foll.

[2] Not a large village but the city of Benares (Kāśī).

[3] Majjhima Nikāya, Vol. II, p. 101.

Prasenajit's visit to the Buddha.

the Teacher why he should be called Sammāsaṁbuddha when Pūraṇa Kassapa, Makkhali Gosāla and Nigaṇṭha Nāthaputta who were older in age, were alive. The Blessed One satisfied the king by saying that one should not neglect a Kṣatriya, Uraga, Agñi and Arahat, although they were younger in age. "Is there any being on earth who is not subject to old age or death?"—was the question put by the Kosalan king to the Buddha who gave a suitable answer.

There was a discussion between Pasenadī and the Buddha regarding soul. 'One loves the soul too much'—this was the topic of discussion.

Even after Pasenadī's initiation, he did not disregard other sādhus and hermits, e.g. the Jaṭilas, the Nigaṇṭhas, the Acelakas or naked ascetics, Ekasātakas and the Paribbājakas. He once asked the Buddha, "who is the foremost among the Arahats"? The Buddha replied, "You are a householder, you find delight in sensual pleasures. It will not be possible for you to understand this question." Thereupon Pasenadī said to the Lord, "Your speech is excellent, You are right." [1]

The Buddha spoke to the Kosalan king about the utility of wealth.

It is stated in the Sumaṅgalavilāsinī that Pasenadī of Kosala gave plenty of land to the brahmin Pokkharasāti, a learned vedic teacher of Ukkaṭṭhanagara, in the kingdom of Kosala. He lived there in ease and comfort (p. 246).

According to the Papañcasūdanī, Buddhaghosa's commentary on the Majjhima Nikāya, a merchant named

[1] Saṁyutta-Nikāya, pt. I, pp. 78–79.

Sudatta was the chief banker of Śrāvastī. He went to the house of his sister at Rājagaha and listened to the teachings of the Buddha. He desired to bring the Buddha to his native city and to serve him to his satisfaction. Unfortunately there was no fit place for the Buddha at Śrāvastī and he determined to build a monastery in the city. This Sudatta was Anāthapiṇḍika.

Buddhaghosa also speaks of Visākhā, the wealthiest woman devotee of the Buddha. She built for the Buddha a monastery called Pubbārāma. He says that she was the daughter of a banker of a city named Bhaddiya in the country of Aṅga and was the daughter-in-law of a banker at Śrāvastī.

Buddhaghosa often mixes up fact and fable without exercising any discrimination. In his Dhammapada-aṭṭhakathā, Vol. I, part II, he records that there lived at Kosāmbi a king named Parantapa. One day he sat under the sun with his pregnant wife who was covered with a red blanket. At that time a bird named Hatthiliṅga taking her to be a lump of flesh, came to her and took her away with its claws. These birds had the strength of five elephants. The queen thought that before it would eat her, she would cry out and it would leave her. It was in the habit of looking back on the track, the queen cried and the bird left her. At that time rain poured heavily and continued throughout the night. Early in the morning, when the sun rose, a son was born to her. A hermit came to the spot where the son was born and saw the queen on the Nigrodha tree which was not far from his hermitage. When the queen introduced herself as a Kṣatriyānī, the hermit brought down the baby from the tree. The queen came to the hermitage of the sage who accompanied her with her infant son. The queen succeeded in tempting him to take her as his spouse and they lived as husband and wife. One day the hermit looked at the stars and saw the star of Parantapa disfigured. He informed her of the death of Parantapa of Kosāmbi. The queen cried and told him, "He is my husband, I am his queen. If my son had lived there, he would have become the king." The hermit assured her that he would help her son to win the kingdom. Her son eventually became king and was known as Udayaṇa. The new king married Sāmāvatī, a daughter of a treasurer of Kosāmbi. Buddhaghosa also records the account of the elopement of Vāsavadattā with Udayaṇa, as we find it in the Svapnavāsavadattā by Bhāṣa. Udayaṇa had another wife named Māgandiyā, the daughter of a brahmin in the kingdom of the Kurūs. (Udena Vatthu, p. 161 foll.)

Account of Anāthapiṇḍika.

According to the Dhammapada-aṭṭhakathā, Anāthapiṇḍika built a vihāra known as Jetavana Vihāra for the Buddha at the expense of 54 koṭis of kahāpaṇa (Catupaṇṇāsa koṭidhanaṁ vissajjetvā, D.P. commentary, P.T.S., Vol. I, pp. 4–5). The great banker first saw the Buddha at Rājagaha in the house of his sister. He was much pleased with the Teacher whom he invited to go to Sāvatthī. He built the Jetavana Vihāra for the Master's residence. The site of the monastery was bought from Prince Jeta and the Buddha stayed there for nineteen years. It was the first vihāra built for the Buddha. In the house of Anāthapiṇḍika, alms were offered daily to two thousand Bhikkhus. Gradually he became poor. A girl of Anāthapiṇḍika's family went to the kingdom of Sātavāhana and there she offered alms to a Bhikkhu with the rice collected from khala. A mahāthera informed king Sātavahāna of it and eventually the girl was made the chief queen of the monarch. (Dhammapada-aṭṭhakathā, Burmese edition, p. 333.)

Account of Bodhirājakumāra.

In his commentary on the Dhammapada, Buddhaghosa narrated a story in which the master-builder of a palace saved his life by flying through the air. It relates that Bodhirājakumāra had a palace built by an engineer, which was unique at that time. The engineer was asked whether he had built a similar palace before. Bodhirājakumāra thought that if the engineer lived, he would build a similar palace and in that case, his building would lose its charm. He decided that he should be killed or his hands and feet be cut off. The engineer came to know of this and in order to save himself, went to the top floor of the building and when he was asked whether he had finished his work, he requested the prince to supply him with some light dry wood. With this he prepared a garuḍa-bird, sufficient for the accommodation of his wife and children. Prince Bodhi guarded the palace in order that the engineer might not go out. When the latter had finished making the bird, he sat within its body with his wife and children, and escaped flying through the window of the palace. (Dhammapada Commentary, Vol. III, p. 134 foll., Bodhirājakumāravatthu.)

Fauna and Flora.

Buddhaghosa well appreciates the beauty of bird-life and the effect of the sweet songs of birds on the human mind. He says when a bird sings a flute-like song after pecking at honey and mangoes, the song throws a sort of Orpheus spell over every one that hears it.[1] He is, however, ready to give credence to fabulous stories of birds. In the Dhammapada-aṭṭhakathā, he makes mention of a bird called Hatthiliṅga which is described as an animal possessing the strength of five elephants. It was in the habit of looking back on the track it had already trodden. (Vol. I, Part II, Udena Vatthu.) His knowledge of the vegetable kingdom is evidenced by his mention of the five classes into which it is divided.[2]

Side-lights on ancient manners.

Incidentally while explaining terms or expressions in the text, he gives us some glimpses into social life in ancient India. Thus he speaks of the tricks performed by jugglers and says that three varieties of them were recognised.[3] He had some knowledge of music, etc., as is clear from his explanations of vetālam and of pekkhaṁ which occur in the Brahmajāla Sutta. The word, pekkhaṁ, is explained by Buddhaghosa as naṭasamajjā, that is, theatrical performances, pekkhaṁ being equivalent to Sanskrit prekṣā. He knew something about dancing and the decorations of scenic requirements for a dance. He knew something about acrobatic feats as is apparent from his explanation of turning over a trapeze.[4]

---

1 Dialogues of the Buddha, pt. I, p. 6 f.n.

2 Ibid., pt. I, p. 15 f.n.

3 Ibid., pt. I, p. 16 f.n.

4 Ibid., pt. I., p. 10, f.n. 10.

Reminiscences of Ceylon.

We may also here refer to certain passages in which Buddhaghosa shows his knowledge of Ceylon. Mention is made of a thera named Mahānāga of Kāḷavallimaṇḍapa and of the bhikkhus who took their abode in the vihāra at Colombotittha, who with minds bent upon Kammaṭṭhāna, walking on foot near the village and taking palmful of water, looking on the roads where quarrelsome and wicked persons, mad elephants, restive horses, etc., were to be found, used to go along their path.[1] Buddhaghosa refers to the story that Thera Mahānāga while going out after finishing his alms-begging in the village of Nakulanagara, saw a therī and requested her to take rice.[2] A reference is made to Abhaya Thera in the Atthasālinī, who was very hospitable to those who could recite the Dīgha Nikāya in the Cetiyapabbata. The story is told of the articles of hospitality having been stolen by thieves.[3] The Atthasālinī also mentions a thera named Piṅgalabuddharakkhita of Ambariya Vihāra who used to preach the Buddhist precepts.[4] A

---

[1] Sāratthapakāsinī (mss.), pp. 132–133. " Evaṁ Kāḷavalli maṇḍapavāsī Mahānāgathero viya-Kaḷamba (Gaḷamba) tittha vihāṛe vassūpagata-bhikkhū viya ca Kammaṭṭhānayutteneva cittena padaṁ uddharanto gāmasamīpaṁ gantvā udakagaṇḍusaṁ katvā vithiyo sallakkhetvā yatthasurā-soṇḍadhuttādayo kalahakārakā caṇḍahatthī assādayo va n'atthi tam vithiṁ paṭipajjati."

[2] Atthasālinī (P.T.S.), p. 399. "....Mahānāgatthero Nakulanagaragāme piṇḍāya caritvā nikkhamanto theriṁ disvā bhattena āpucchi."

[3] Atthasālinī, p.399. " Uppannalābhathāvarakaraṇe Dīghabhāṇakā Abhayattherassa hatthato paṭisanthāraṁ labhitvā Cetiyapabbate corehi bhaṇḍakassa aviluttabhāve vatthuṁ kathetabbaṁ."

[4] Ibid., p. 103, " Ambariyavihāravāsī-Piṅgalabuddharakkhitattherassa santike sikkhāpadāni gahetvā ....."

reference is made to a sinless thera living at Cittalapabbata, who had as his attendant an old recluse. One day while the attendant was walking behind the thera with alms-bowl and robes, he spoke to the thera thus, "Venerable Sir, how are the Ariyas"? The answer was that the Ariyas were a people very difficult to be known.[1] Mention is also made of Cakkana Upāsaka of the island of Ceylon.[2]

In the Sāratthapakāsinī, it is stated that in the island of Ceylon, in the rest-houses of different villages, there was no seat where a Bhikkhu taking his gruel did not obtain Arahatship. Buddhaghosa further refers to the town of Icchaṅgala near which a temporary residence of stone was built, where the king of righteousness dwelt as long as he lived.[4] In the Sāratthapakāsinī by Buddhaghosa, it is stated that one day in the court-yard of Mahācetiya of Laṅkā, young bhikkhus were engaged in getting their lessons by heart, behind them young bhikkhunis were listening to the repetition, one of the bhikkhus having extended his hands that touched a bhikkhunī became a householder or layman.[5] Buddhaghosa in his Atthasālinī, a commentary

---

1 Atthasālinī, p. 350, "Cittalapabbatavāsike kira khīnāsavattherassa upaṭṭhāko buddhapabbajito ekadivasaṁ therena saddhiṁ piṇḍāyacaritvā therassa pattacīvaraṁ gahetvā piṭṭhito āgacchanto theraṁ pucchi: 'Bhante ariyā nāma kidisā ti? .... dujjanā āvuso ariyā."

2 Ibid., p. 103, ".... Sīhaladīpe Cakkana-upāsakassa viya."

3 Sāratthapakāsinī, p. 131.

4 Cf. also the Chapter XXVI which deals with the consecration of Maricavaṭṭi Vihāra as described in the Mahāvaṁsa. "Icchānaṅgala-vanasaṇḍe Sīlakkhaṇḍa vāraṁ bandhitvā samādhikontaṁ ussāpetva sabbaññutañānasaraṁ parivattayamāno dhammarājā yathābhirucitena vihārena viharati."

5 Sāratthapakāsinī, p. 137. Mahācetiyaṅgaṇa appears to be the court-yard of

on the Dhammasaṅgaṇi, refers to Penaṁbaṅgaṇa, a town in Ceylon, where there is a perpetual flow of charity, etc.[1]

The Visuddhimagga, the monumental work of Buddhaghosa, abounds in references to Ceylon. Mention is made of Thera Mahā Tissa of the Cetiyapabbata who was in the habit of coming from Cetiyapabbata to Anurādhapura for alms.[2] Two members of a family are mentioned in the Visuddhimagga as coming out of Anurādhapura and gradually obtaining ordination at Thūpārāma.[3] A thera named Nāga of Karaḷiyagiri gave a discourse on dhātukathā to the bhikkhus.[4] A reference is made to a thera named Cūḷābhaya who was versed in the three piṭakas, and learnt the Aṭṭhakathā.[5] The Visuddhimagga mentions Anurādhapura[6] several times.

Buddhaghosa's knowledge of Anatomy.

Buddhaghosa had a fair knowledge of anatomy, as is apparent from his account of the thirty-two parts of the body, recorded in his Visuddhimagga.[7] According to

Mahācetiya of Anurādhapur in Ceylon. It occurs in many places in the Mahāvaṁsa. For its description see Parker's "Ruined cities of Ceylon." ". Atthepanasati pi sappāya sappāyaṁ pariganetvā sappāya pariggaṇhanaṁ sappāya saṁpajaññaṁ tatrāyaṁ nayo : Mahācetiyaṅgane kira daharabhikkhū sajjhāyaṁ gaṇhanti. Tesaṁ piṭṭhipasse daharā bhikkhuniyo dhammaṁ suvanti. Tatreko daharo hatthaṁ pasārento kāyasaṁsaggaṁ patvā teneva kāranena gihījāto."

1 Atthasālinī, P.T.S., p. 399.

2 Visuddhimagga, Vol. I., p. 20, 'Cetiyapabbatavāsī Mahā Tissattheroviya ... theraṁ ..... Cetiyapabbatā Anurādhapuraṁ piṇḍācāratthaya.....

3 Ibid., Vol. I, p. 90. 4 Ibid., Vol. I, p. 96.

5 Ibid., Vol. I, p. 96. 6 Ibid., Vol. I, p. 72.

7 Vol. I (P.T.S.), pp. 249–265. See also Visuddhimagga, Vol. I, pp. 353–363. Cf. Paramatthajotikā on the Khuddakapāṭha, Vol. I., pp. 41–68; cf. Sammohavinodanī (Sinhalese edition), pp. 49–63.

Thūpārāma Dagoba.

him, the human body is composed of 32 things which he named as impurities, viz: kesa, loma, nakha, danta, taca, maṁsa, nahāru, aṭṭhi, aṭṭhimiñjaṁ, vakkaṁ, hadayaṁ, yakanaṁ, kilomakaṁ, pihakaṁ, papphāsaṁ, antaṁ, antaguṇaṁ, udariyaṁ, karīsaṁ, matthaluṅgaṁ, pittaṁ, semhaṁ, pubbo, lohitaṁ, sedo, medo, assu, vasā, keḷo, singhāṇikā, lasikā and muttaṁ.

We are told that *Kesa* is hair which is black and which grows on the head. It has been described as an impurity in colour, in form and in smell. We are further told that a person naturally dislikes a pot of nicely-cooked rice or rice-gruel if he sees anything like a hair in it.

Loma means hair of the body. Naturally it is of mixed colour, a combination of black and reddish-yellow. It grows on the skin of the whole body except the head where hairs grow.

Nakhā are the nails of the twenty fingers. They are white in colour, in shape they are like maccha-sakalikā (fish-scales).

Dantā (teeth) are naturally thirty-two in number for those who have got a full set of them, but occasionally there are exceptions. The four middle teeth of the lower gum are like the seed of a gourd sown on a ball of soft clay in a row, one after the other. On each side of the four middle teeth, there are two that have one root and one top and in size they resemble the buds of the Mallikā flower. On both sides of these two teeth again, there are two which have two roots and two tops and in shape they resemble the support of a cart. Next, on each side of the above two, there are two pairs of teeth having three roots and three tops and on both sides of the two pairs of teeth, there are two other pairs having four roots and four tops.

Taca means skin of the body. It covers the whole body. The colour of the skin is called *Chavi*. If the skin of the body be so contracted as to form one lump, it will resemble the stone of a plum. The taca is white in colour. Its whiteness is seen when it is burst open by the heat of the fire. In shape, it is like that of the body. The skin of the toes is in shape like a scabbard. The skin of the upper part of the feet is like a wooden slipper covered with skin. The skin of the knee is like a rice-plate or palm-leaf. The skin of the thigh is like a bag full of rice. The skin of the hind parts resembles a bag of a water-man, full of water. The skin of the back is like a wooden board covered with skin.

Maṁsa means flesh and is composed of nine hundred lumps. All the lumps of flesh are red like the Kiṁsuka flower. The flesh of the knee is like a rice-plate or palm-leaf. The flesh of the hinder parts is like the top of a furnace. The flesh of the back is like a lump of jaggery. The side-flesh is like a mud-plaster over the belly of an idol. The flesh of the breast resembles a covered lump of clay. The flesh of the arms is like the flesh of two big mice.

Nahāru denotes the muscles which are nine hundred in number. All the muscles are white in colour, and are of various shapes There are twenty big muscles, five on the left, five on the right, five on the back and five in the front, which come down from the top of the neck and spread all over the body. There are ten muscles in each hand, five in the front and five at the back. So also in the case of the feet. There are sixty big muscles in the whole body and they are known as supporters of the body. There are smaller muscles which resemble thread-ropes. There are still smaller muscles which are like the putilatā (cocculus cordifolius). There are still smaller muscles which are like the strings of big lutes. The smallest muscles are like thick threads. The muscles of the different parts of the body have different shapes.

Aṭṭhi means bone. Besides the thirty-two bones of the teeth, there are three hundred bones in the human body including sixty-four bones of the hands, sixty-two of the feet, sixty-four short bones mixed with flesh, two bones of the palms of the hands, four bones of the heels, two leg bones, two knee bones, two thigh bones, two waist bones, eighteen back bones, twenty-four side bones, fourteen chest bones, one bone of the heart, two eye bones, two bones of the koṭṭha, two bones of the arms, four bones of the forearms, seven bones of the neck, two bones of the jaw, one of the nose, two collar bones, two ear bones, one bone of the forehead, one bone of the top of the head, one bone of the head and nine bones of the skull. The different shapes of the bones are described and we are told that the bones of the head rest upon the bones of the neck which are supported by the bones of the back which again are sustained by the bones of the waist which on their part, rest upon the bones of the thighs, which again are supported by the bones of the knee, which again lean upon the bones of the heels which again rest on the bones of the feet and so on.

Aṭṭhimiñjā—It means marrow of three hundred bones. Its colour is white. The shape of the marrow is like that of the bone in which it lies.

Vakkaṁ—It is a pair of lumps of flesh combined in one stalk. Its colour is slightly red. Its form is like that of two mangoes joined together in one stalk. It remains all round the flesh of the heart. The two lumps of flesh are connected together by the big nerve coming down from the neck; the big nerve has been divided into two parts.

Hadayaṁ—It means flesh of the heart (hadaya-maṁsa). It is red in colour like the back of a lotus-leaf. Its shape is like that of a lotus-leaf turned upside down. Its outward appearance is polished but its inward appearance is like that of the kosātakī fruit. The heart of a wise man is open and the heart of the fool is not open. Inside the heart there is a hole aṣ big as a nut, which contains a half-handful of blood. Mind and mind-consciousness depend upon that blood which is red in case of passionate beings and black in case of hot-tempered persons, in case of fools it is like the water used for washing meat, in case of persons given to much disputation, its colour is like that of kulatta pea soup; in case of persons having faith, its colour is like that of the kaṇikāra flower; in case of persons who are wise, it is clear and free from impurities. The heart is situated between the two breasts.

Yakanaṁ—It consists of a pair of lumps of flesh. It is red in colour like that of the back of the leaf of the Lily. In shape it appears like the leaves of kovilāra. The fools have got one big liver. The wise have got two or three small livers. It stands between the two breasts, close to the right one.

Kilomako—It is of two kinds, covered and uncovered flesh. Both of them are white in colour like pieces of white cloth. The covered one is on the upper part of the body, the other exists both in the upper and lower parts of the body. The covered one covers hadayaṁ and vakkaṁ and the uncovered one extends all over the body just below the skin encircling the flesh.

Pihakaṁ—It is the tongue of the stomach. It is blue in colour like niggundi flower. Its size is seven inches. It exists on the left side of the heart, close to the topmost part of the flesh of the stomach. If it comes out of its place due to beating, the creature dies.

Papphāsaṁ—It is the flesh of the lungs divided into thirty-two pieces; in colour it is like a fig which is very ripe. In shape it is like a cake which is not properly cut. The interior of it is dry and it exists between the two breasts, hanging over the heart and liver and covering them.

Antaṁ—It means the intestine. The size of a male's intestine is thirty-two cubits in length. It remains coiled in twenty-one places. In colour, it is as white as white pebbles. Its shape is like that of a headless snake coiled in a pot of blood. It stretches from the neck to the excretal passage (kasiramagga).

Antaguṇaṁ—It means the small intestines. They spring up from the place where the larger intestines remain coiled up. They are as white as roots washed in water. In shape they are like the root.

Udariyam—It means the things accumulated in the stomach by eating, drinking, fasting and so forth. In colour udariyam is like the colour of food which has gone into the stomach. In shape it is like loosely tied up rice in a water strainer. It remains inside the stomach which is like the bubble in the middle of a wet cloth when twisted by both hands. Outwardly the stomach is very smooth. Its inside is rough like a soiled pavāraka flower. There are thirty-two kinds of germs in the stomach such as gaṇḍuppādakā, takkoṭṭakā, etc. If these germs do not get food, they jump up and bite the heart-flesh. They move about in the stomach. They are as ugly as the earth-worms moving about in the rotten rubbish heaps when wetted by rain-water. The food which is put into the stomach is utilised in five ways, one portion of it is eaten up by the germs, one portion is burnt by the fire of the stomach, one portion turns into urine, one portion turns into excreta and the remaining portion is reduced to juice which produces flesh and blood.

Karisaṁ—It means excrement. In colour it is like that of the food put into the stomach. Its shape is like that of its place of origin.

Matthaluṅgaṁ—It means marrows inside the skull of the head, white in colour, and they are like a lump of mushrooms or like bad milk which is not properly changed into curd. The shape of the marrows is like that of the skull of the head. They are like four balls of cakes sewn together.

Pittaṁ—There are two kinds of pitta (bile), one is baddhapitta (closed bile) and the other is avaddhapitta (open bile). In colour, the former one is like that of thick oil or honey, the colour of the latter is like that of an old ākuli flower. The shape of both of them is like that of the pot in which they remain. The baddhapitta is in the upper part of the body and the avaddhapitta remains in both the upper and the lower parts. The avaddhapitta exists like a drop of oil in water in all parts of the body except the fleshless portions of kesa, loma, danta, nakha and dry hard skin. If the avaddhapitta be in excess, the eyes become yellow and they roll, the body shakes and feels an aching sensation. The baddhapitta exists in a bag of bile, which is like the cover of mahākosātakī and which lies between the heart and the lungs, just by the side of the liver. If this be in excess, the beings become mad, the mind loses its sobriety and the beings lost to all sense of shame, do what they should not do, say what they should not say, and think what they should not think.

Semhaṁ—It means phlegm. There is a bowl-full of phlegm in the human body. It is white in colour and its shape is like that of the pot in which it lies. It grows in the upper part of the body and it remains inside the stomach. When food goes into the stomach, some portion of the phlegm becomes displaced but it again comes back to its former position.

Pubbo—It means pus, and consists of rotten blood. Its colour is like that of an old leaf. Its shape is like that of the pot in which it is contained. It appears in all the parts of the body. It has no definite place of origin. It appears in boils which arise owing to accumulation of blood in the parts of the body, which are hurt or burnt.

Lohita—It means blood. There are two kinds of blood, sannicitalohita (accumulated blood) and saṁsaranalohita (running blood). The colour of the former is like the colour of the very thick juice of lac and the colour of the latter is like that of the clear juice of lac. They take the shape of the vessel in which they are contained. The accumulated blood can be found in the upper part of the body, and the other, in both the parts. Saṁsaranalohita passes through the veins all over the body except the fleshless portion of kesa, loma, danta, nakha and dry hard skin, and the sannicitalohita is below the liver, and bowl-full in quantity. It wets the heart, the kidney and the lungs, and if it does not do so, creatures become thirsty.

Sedo—It means the water which comes out of the pores of the skin. Its colour is like that of clear sesamum oil and it grows in both the parts of the body. It has no definite place of origin.

Medo—It means thick oil. Its colour is like that of powdered turmeric. Its shape is like that of a yellow rag placed in the midst of flesh and skin of a fat being and in case of a lean person, its shape is like that of a double or triple yellow rag placed close to the flesh of the knee, thigh and collar bone, and flesh of the belly. It grows in the upper and lower parts of the body.

Assu—It means water coming out of the eyes. Its colour is like that of clear sesamum oil. Its shape is like that of the vessel in which it is contained and it exists in the upper part of the body. It remains in the sockets of the eyes. It does not always remain there. When beings become delighted at heart, and laugh and also when they weep and cry, when they take unsuitable food, and when their eyes are hurt by dust, smoke, etc., then the eyes become full of tears which trickle down.

Vasā—It means thin oil Its colour is like that of cocoanut oil. Its shape is like that of a drop of oil in water. It exists in the upper and lower parts of the body and it is found chiefly in the palms and backs of the hands, in the lower parts of the feet, in the nostrils, on forehead and shoulders, when heated by the rays of the sun or by fire, etc.

Keḷo—It means saliva. It is white like foam. Its shape is like that of the place in which it is found. It remains in the upper part of the body. It remains on the tongue by the side of both the cheeks.

Siṅghānikā—It means the mucus of the brain. Its colour is like that of the marrow of a young palm. Its shape is like that of the vessel in which it is contained. It fully occupies the nose-holes. It does not always remain in the nose-holes but when creatures cry or when by unsuitable food or climate, the elements of the body are agitated, then the rotten brain comes out through the holes of the palate and accumulates there.

Lasikā—It means the slippery dirt inside the joints of the body. Its colour is like that of the kaṇikāra flower. Its shape is like that of the place in which it exists. It remains in the upper and lower parts of the body. It occurs in the eighty joints of the body and oils them. If this be small in quantity, a person loses his activity and feels tired after walking one or two yojanas. But one becomes active and does not get tired after walking if this element be large in quantity.

Muttaṁ—It means urine. Its colour is like that of the water in which bean is washed. Its shape is like that of water inside a jar which is turned upside down. It remains in the lower part of the body and in the bladder. Although there appears to be no entrance to the bladder, yet it enters into it, and the path by which it comes out of the bladder, is wide.

CHAPTER VII

THE PHILOSOPHY OF BUDDHAGHOSA

The early philosophical training of Buddhaghosa.

The accounts of the life of Buddhaghosa before he adopted the Buddhist faith, depict him as a person well versed in the Brahmanical lore, and following the usage of his time, wandering about in the country as a sophist. No doubt he studied philosophical treatises but his philosophic genius remained latent till it was roused by the forceful arguments of the Thera Revata who is said to have defeated him in a philosophical discussion, with the result that he became a pupil of that great sage. With the thera, it is said, he studied the Pāli Tripiṭaka, which roused in him a burning desire to know the religion of the Buddha, which eventually made him a devoted student of Buddhist Philosophy.

His connection with the school of Patañjali.

A tradition tells us that he was an adherent of the system of Patañjali and it seems to be substantiated by his own words in the commentaries. Buddhaghosa is strong, throughout his works, in his attacks on Pakativāda, i. e. the Sāṅkhya and the Yoga systems which believe in the dual principles of Puruṣa and Prakriti. He shows an extravagant zeal for differentiating the Buddhist conception of Avijjā from the Prakritivadin's conception of Prakriti as the root cause of things,[1] and the Buddhist conception of Nāmarūpa from the outsider's conception of Puruṣa and Prakriti. He betrays nevertheless his previous predilection for the Sāṅkhya and the Yoga systems. His conception of Nāmarūpa is very much like the Sāṅkhya conception of Puruṣa and Prakriti. He uses the very simile of the blind and the lame by which the two conceptions are illustrated.[2] It might be argued that Buddhaghosa based his conception on the authority of the earlier Buddhist thinkers, notably Nāgasena and Aṣvaghosa.[3] But who can deny that the Buddhist thinkers, too, were greatly influenced by the Sāṅkhya line of thinking? Indeed, taking into consideration all available evidence we cannot but agree with M. Oltramare in maintaining that the Buddhist conception of Nāmarūpa was from a certain date steadily tending towards the Sāṅkhya conception of Puruṣa and Prakriti. It would be travelling too far from our immediate object to institute an enquiry into the relationship between the Buddhist Philosophy and the mode of self-realization on the one hand, and the Yoga system on the other. Accepting as a working hypothesis that the relationship is in many respects close, it requires no effort of the imagination to realize how Buddhaghosa easily passed from the old to the new.

---

1 "Kasmā pan'ettha avijjā ādito vuttā? Kiṁ, pakativādinaṁ pakati viya, avijjā pi akāranaṁ mūlakāranaṁ lokassāti"? Visuddhimagga, Vol. II, p. 525.

2 Cf. the passage quoted in Vyāṣa's commentary on Yoga Sutra, III, 44.

3 Paramatthajotikā, II, Vol. I, p. 169. "Athavā sante na kurute iti sante na sevatī ti attho, yathā 'rājānaṁ sevatī' ti etasmim atthe 'rājānaṁ pakurute' ti saddavidū mantenti." It is an application of the rule of Pāṇini, I, 3-32.

Buddhist influence on Buddhaghosa.

The Brāhmaṇic spirit and the Vedantic ideas imbibed and acquired by him in his boyhood ceased to influence him in his youth when he came to be interested in Buddhism. He entertained so high an esteem for the Buddha that commenting on the Dīgha Nikāya, he explains the Great One as Mahā Brahmā.[1] The effect of the Buddhistic influence on Buddhaghosa showed itself in his philosophical treatise which he called Ñānodaya or the 'Awakening of Intellect.' But at the time Buddhaghosa flourished, "the philosophical culture of Buddhist India was expressing itself in Sanskrit. In the literature of that culture there is ample testimony, in such works as survive, to reveal developments in logic and in metaphysic."[2] The patient work of many centuries left behind by India's introspective geniuses is a mine of knowledge, yet to be explored. In this field Buddhist thinkers have laboured with acumen and patient diligence. "The more we advance in Central Asiatic research," wrote the late Prof. R. Pischel, "the clearer it appears that, for a great portion of the Orient, Buddhism was not less a vehicle of culture than Christianity has been for the Occident." "While Buddhism," he goes on to say, "as a religion gains (by that research) ever in value, as a philosophy it sinks ever deeper."[4]

The whole of Buddhist Philosophy along with Buddhist

---

[1] Dialogues of the Buddha, pt. I, p. 24 f.n.

[2] Buddhism by Mrs. Rhys Davids, p. 44.

[3] Buddhist Psychology (Quest Series), by Mrs. Rhys Davids, p. vi.

[4] Buddhism by Mrs. Rhys Davids, pp. 30–31.

religion rests on a psychological basis.[1] Yet more marked is the psychological advance met with in the works of Buddhaghosa.[2] He expounds his psychology in terms of the five aggregate division.[3] Here the five aggregates are—material qualities, feeling, sense-perception, complexes of consciousness or co-efficients, and, fifthly consciousness itself.[4]

We shall try first of all to give in brief an idea of the psychological concepts of the Buddha.

Citta.

According to Buddhaghosa, the meaning of the word 'citta' is that which cognises external objects. Its characteristic is recognition. It is presupposed by every sense-conception. Whatever one sees through his eyes, hears through his ears, smells through his nose, tastes through his tongue, touches through his body and cognises through his mind—all these he recognises by his citta.[5] Mind by itself is connected with emptiness and absence of a living entity. After sense-perception, it recognises the objects and receives them and manifests the state of such reception. In the absence of mind there is no visual or other cognition.[6] Citta and Cetasika are described as 'the shell and the contents of a sphere.'[7] Mrs. Rhys

---

[1] Buddhist Psychology (Quest Series), by Mrs. Rhys Davids, p. vi.

[2] Buddhism by Mrs. Rhys Davids, p. 63.

[3] Buddhist Psychology (Quest Series), p. 174. [4] Ibid., p. 40.

[5] Atthasālinī (P.T.S.) p. 112. "Yaṁ cakkhunā rūpaṁ passati .... yaṁ sotena saddaṁ suṇāti, ghānena gandhaṁ ghāyati, jivhāya rasaṁ sāyati, kāyena phoṭṭhabbaṁ phusati, manasā dhammaṁ vijānāti tam viññāṇena vijānātīti."

[6] Ibid., p. 263. "Manodhātuniddesa sabhāvasuññatanissattaṭṭhena mano yeva dhātu .... sā cakkhuviññāṇādīnaṁ anantaraṁ rūpādivijānanalakkhaṇā rūpādisampaṭicchanarasā tathābhāvapaccupaṭṭhānā cakkhuviññāṇādi-apagāmanapadaṭṭhānā."

[7] Mrs. Rhys Davids' Buddhist Psychology (Quest Series), p. 8.

Davids explains the term Citta as consciousness (mind, 'heart,' intelligence).[1] "Cittaṁ iti pi mano iti pi viññānaṁ." On the above passage Mrs. Rhys Davids remarks thus, "In commenting, centuries later, on this passage, Buddhaghosa, the greatest of the scholastics, calls all three a name for the manāyatana or sphere of cognition. Elsewhere the first two of the three terms are used as practically coincident, but this is the only passage known to me where all three are so represented."[2] We quite agree with Mrs. Rhys Davids on this point. She tells us further that the meaning of these three terms is practically the same.[3]

According to Spence Hardy, it is by the action of the mind upon the power of reflection that thought is produced. The principal faculty connected with cetanā is the mind. Citta is ārammanaṁ cintetīti cittaṁ. We agree with Mr. S. Z. Aung when he speaks of the word cinteti thus: It is "used in its most comprehensive sense of vijānāti (to know) Mind is, then, ordinarily defined as that which is conscious of an object. This is called the kattusādhana definition, or definition by which an agency is attributed to the thing denoted by the term."[5]

It is to be noted that citta and viññāna convey the same meaning. Viññāna simply conveys the idea of the 'totality of consciousness.' It also means thought, mind.[6]

In the opinion of Ledi Sadaw, "Mind, mental factors,

---

[1] Mrs. Rhys Davids' Buddhist Psychology (Quest Series), p. 6.

[2] Ibid., pp. 17–18. [3] Ibid., p. 18.

[4] Spence Hardy, Manual of Buddhism, pp. 420–421.

[5] Aung, Compendium of Philosophy, p. 2.

[6] Childers' Pāli Dictionary, p. 576.

material quality, nibbāṇa are just such abstruse, subtle, recondite matters. For the untrained, who are without training of mind and understanding, and who are unable to suspend even for a moment the notion of 'person,' 'being,' 'self' (soul), 'living thing,' the real nature of these phenomena are beyond the average range of their ken. But these matters are within the range of the intelligence which knows by way of intuition. For those whose knowledge has been abundantly trained in the doctrines of the intuitively wise Ariyan philosophers, even their inferential knowledge may be said to partake of the nature of intuitive knowledge, since it invariably leads to the latter kind." Sadaw further remarks that "they whose knowledge has not penetrated the fact of the arising and ceasing of the material qualities, are blind to that arising and ceasing; they only see a continuous and a static condition in those phenomena. They consider their own mind as a permanent something. They conceive the selfsame mind moving about here and there within the body. The selfsame mind in the morning, the selfsame mind at noon, and at eventide the selfsame mind ....what they neither know nor see is conditioned genesis of mind (citto)." [1]

We know that finally mind is a source of consciousness or as Sadaw puts it 'representative consciousness.'

Phassa.

According to Buddhaghosa, 'Phassa' means contact. [2] Its characteristic is touching, its function being to bring one in contact with

[1] 'Some points in Buddhist Doctrine,' J.P.T.S., 1913-14, p. 155.

[2] Atthasālini, p. 136. "Yo phusanakavasena uppanno phasso so phassoti."

an external object, its effect is to bring together. The object which comes in its way causes 'Phassa.' It is formless. It exists by sticking to some object. The relation between Phassa and its object is the relation between eye and form, ear and sound, mind and object of thought.[1] One of the Saṅkhāras is Phassa. Mrs. Rhys Davids says, "Phassa (contact)......is generalised to include all receptive experience, sensory as well as ideational, and to represent the essential antecedent and condition of all feeling......phusati, phoṭṭhabbaṁ (to touch, the tangible) are specialised to express the activity of one of the senses."[2]

It is stated in the Visuddhimagga, Chapter XVII, that Phassa is due to six āyatanas. Phassa is of six kinds:—

1. Cakkhusaṁphassa;
2. Sotasaṁphassa;
3. Ghānasaṁphassa;
4. Jivhāsaṁphassa;
5. Kāyasaṁphassa; and
6. Manosaṁphassa.

By Phassa, Mr. S. Z. Aung understands thus, "First of all, the subject is aware of the presence of an object. And in the case of the type of thought under discussion the object is either an agreeable sight, sound, smell, taste, touch or concrete mental object (dhammārammaṇa)—agreeable in the sense that it is desired by the subject (iṭṭhāram-

[1] Visuddhimagga (P.T.S.), p. 463. "....arūpadhammo pi samāno, ārammaṇe phusanākāren'va pavattati. Ekadesena ca analliyamāno pi, rūpaṁ viya cakkhu, saddo viya ca sotam, cittaṁ ārammaṇañ ca sanghaṭṭeti."

[2] Mrs. Rhys Davids' A Buddhist Manual of Psychological Ethics, pp. lv–lvi.

maṇa). This awareness of the objective presentation is termed contact (phassa)."[1]

Vedanā. According to Buddhaghosa, Vedanākkhandha means whatever has the characteristic of being felt; it consists of three classes according to origin—kusala, akusala and avyākata though these are of the same nature on account of their being felt. According to its nature, Vedanā is of five kinds, viz. sukhaṁ, dukkhaṁ, somanassaṁ, domanassaṁ and upekkhā.[2]

Vedanā is also divided into six kinds, viz. cakkhusaṁpassajā sotaghānajivhākāyamanosampassajā-Vedana. As these six Vedanās are connected with the eighty-nine cittas, they are said to be divided into eighty-nine. 'Phassa' (contact) is the cause of Vedanā.

In eight different ways, Phassa becomes the cause of the first five kinds of Vedanā. The eight ways are sahajāta (which comes into existence together with it), aññamañña (mutual), nissaya (support), vipāka (consequence), āhāra (nutriment), sampajutta (connected), atthi (existence) and avigata (that which is not gone). Phassa alone is the cause of the remaining ones. Vedanā is also the cause of taṇhā (desire).[3]

Spence Hardy[4] says that Vedanā or sensation is of six kinds. It is produced by communication with that which is

---

[1] Compendium of Philosophy, p. 14.

[2] Visuddhimagga, Vol. II, p. 460.
"Vedayati vedayatīti kho āvuso, tasmā vedanātivuccati."

[3] Visuddhimagga, Vol. II, p. 567—Phassapaccayā vedanā, vedanāpaccayā taṇhā.

[4] Manual of Buddhism, p. 418.

agreeable (kusala), disagreeable (akusala) and avyākata (indifferent). He is of opinion that joy arises when an agreeable thing or object is seen. There is "aversion" when a disagreeable object or thing is seen and there is indifference when an object is seen which is neither agreeable nor disagreeable.

Vedanā, according to Ledi Sadaw, is feeling. He puts it thus, "Given the contact, an act of disagreeable feeling is manifested: this is feeling" (vedanā).[1]

According to Mr. S. Z. Aung, "Vedanā includes such emotions as joy and grief. It covers all kinds of feeling, physical and mental. Vedanā is either kāyika or mānasika. Under the aspect of feeling, Vedanā is either pleasure or pain or neither pain nor pleasure."[2]

Viññānakkhandha.

Viññānakkhandha means all things which have the characteristic of knowing. Viññāṇa, citta and mano convey the same meaning. According to its characteristic, it is of one kind, and according to its origin, it is of three kinds, viz. kusala, akusala and avyākata. Various kinds of kusala, akusala and avyākata have been discussed; kusala is divided into kāmāvacarakusala, rūpāvacarakusala, arūpāvacarakusala and lokuttara. Akusala is principally divided into three according to its origin from lobha, dosa and moha, and avyākata is divided into two classes, viz. vipāka, and kiriyā. Lokuttara is divided into four according to four maggas, and it is again divided into four according to four phalas. A de-

[1] Some points in Buddhist doctrine, J.P.T.S., 1913-14, p. 148.

[2] Compendium of Philosophy, p. 14.

tailed account of the divisions and sub-divisions of terms connected with Viññāṇakkhandha has been noted in the Visuddhimagga.[1]

According to R. C. Childers, Viññāṇa is one of the khandhas. It means intelligence, knowledge, consciousness, thought and mind. He further tells us that "Viññāṇa as the thinking part of the individual is the most important of the five khandhas, and if any one khandha can be said to constitute the individual it is this. In Buddha's words, by the destruction of Mind, the whole being perishes."[2]

Under Viññāṇa or consciousness we have (1) Cakkhuviññāṇa or eye consciousness, (2) Sotaviññāṇa or ear consciousness, (3) Ghānaviññāṇa or nose consciousness, (4) Jivhāviññāṇa or tongue consciousness, (5) Kāyaviññāṇa or body consciousness, (6) Maṇoviññāṇa or mind consciousness.

According to Ledi Sadaw, Viññāṇa or consciousness is "the specific awareness of the material quality (rūpa) called heat." "There is also, through that material quality, a touching, an impressing, a colliding with the sensitive skin" (kāya).[3]

According to Mr. S. Z. Aung, "consciousness may be tentatively defined as the relation between ārammaṇika and ārammaṇa." The object of consciousness is, in his opinion, either object of sense or object of thought. The former subdivides itself into five classes and the latter consists of five sub-classes of which citta is one.[4]

---

[1] Vol. II, pp. 452-460. [2] Childers' Pāli Dictionary, pp 576-577.
[3] Some points in Buddhist Doctrine, J.P.T.S., 1913-14, p. 148.
[4] Compendium of Philosophy, pp. 2-3.

Saññākkhandha.

All things which have the characteristic of perception are termed Saññākkhandha. Saññākkhandha is of three kinds—kusala, akusala and avyākata. Saññā cannot exist without Viññāṇa. Hence we find the same kinds of Saññā as Viññāṇa. The difference lies in the fact that Saññā is only perception of external appearance of an object while Viññāṇa means thorough knowledge of the thing.[1]

According to Mrs. Rhys Davids, "Saññā is not limited to sense-perception, but includes perceiving of all kinds. Our own term 'perception' is similarly elastic." In editing the second book of the Abhidhamma Piṭaka, Mrs. Rhys Davids "found a classification distinguishing between Saññā as cognitive assimilation on occasion of sense, and Saññā as cognitive assimilation of ideas by way of naming. The former is called perception of resistance, or opposition (paṭighasaññā). This, writes Buddhaghosa, is perception on occasion of sight, hearing, etc., when consciousness is aware of the impact of impressions; of external things as different, we might say. The latter is called perception of the equivalent word, or name (adhivacanasaññā) and is exercised by the sensus communis (mano)."[2]

Spence Hardy says, "Saññākkhandha or perceptions are six in number. When an object is seen, whether it be green or red, there is the perception that it is of that parti-

---

[1] Visuddhimagga, Vol. II, p. 462, "....Na hi taṁ viññāṇaṁ atthi yaṁ saññāya vippayuttaṁ, tasmā yattako viññāṇassa bhedo, tattako saññāyāti. Sā pan' esā evaṁ viññāṇena samappabhedā pi lakkhaṇādito sabbā va sañjānanalakkhaṇā."

[2] Buddhist Psychology (Quest Series), pp 49–50.

cular colour. So also when any sound is heard, whether it be from the drum or any other instrument, there is the perception that it is such a sound ; when there is any smell, whether it be agreeable or disagreeable, there is the perception that it is such a smell......"[1]

According to Childers,[2] Saññā means perception. Saññākkhandha is the third khandha. It is subdivided into six :—

1. Cakkhusampassajjāsaññā.
2. Sotasampassajjāsaññā.
3. Ghānasampassajjāsaññā.
4. Jivhāsampassajjāsaññā.
5. Kāyasampassajjāsaññā.
6. Manosampassajjāsaññā.

According to Mr. S. Z. Aung, the term "perception must be understood in the widest significance of the term, somewhat after the manner of Descartes, Malebranche, Locke, Leibnitz and others, before its limitation by Reid. Saññā, in Buddhist psychology, means the awareness of the marks, real or imaginary, by which an object either of sense or thought is or may hereafter be recognised."[3]

Saṅkhārakhandha.

Thirty-six kinds of Saṅkhāra arise from Kāmāvacarapaṭhamakusala and the same number arises from Kāmāvacaradutiyakusala. The same number without amoha, arises from Kāmāvacaratatiyakusala and so on. Seventeen kinds of Saṅkhāra arise from paṭhamaakusala. The same number with Saṅkhāra

[1] Manual of Buddhism, p. 419. [2] Childers' Pali Dictionary, p. 457.
[3] Compendium of Philosophy, pp. 15–16.

arises from dutiyaakusala and the same number without micchādiṭṭhi arises from the third and so on. (Visuddhimagga, Vol. II, pp. 462–472.)

A word is necessary to bring out the significance of the term 'Saṅkhāra.' It means aggregation. The essential characteristic of a Saṅkhāra is 'cetayita,' being work of mind. According to Dr. S. N. Das Gupta, "It is called Saṅkhāra because it synthesises the conglomerated (Saṅkhataṁ abhisaṅkharonti). It is thus a synthetic function which synthesises the passive rūpa, saññā, saṅkhāra and viññāṇa elements." (A History of Indian Philosophy, by Surendra Nath Das Gupta, M.A., Ph.D., p. 96.)

Abhisaṅkhāra is used as a synonym of Saṅkhāra as Childers points out in his Pāli Dictionary. Saṅkhārakhandha has good many points in common with those of Paṭiccasamuppāda. "Both are referred to mind; on the one hand, the Saṅkhāras of the Paṭiccasamuppāda are said to be good and bad cetanās, on the other hand, those of the khandha are said to be mental conditions." (R. C. Childers, Pāli Dictionary, p. 455.)

It has been interpreted as matter, karma, etc. "In some cases, sentient beings are included under the term saṅkhāra, in others the terms satta and saṅkhāra are distinctly opposed." "The fourth khandha known as saṅkhārakkhandha," says Childers, "has a somewhat different meaning. Here the aggregations are certain properties and faculties of the sentient being, fifty-two in number." [1]

---

[1] Childers' Pāli Dictionary, p. 453–455.

According to Mr. S. Z. Aung, Saṅkhārakkhandha means 'the group of volitions and other associated factors.'[1]

Saṅkhāra is that which is determined, conditioned and acted upon. Saṅkhāra is synonymous with Karma and is chiefly applied to Cetanā but is extended secondarily to the properties concomitant with the Cetanā.[2]

Kern says, "Saṅkhāras are affections, temporary mental or moral dispositions, having their motive in Vedanā." "The aggregation of the five khandhas constitute the puggala (puggala)."[3]

It is stated in the Visuddhimagga, Chapter XIV, that under the Saṅkhārakkhandha, we have fifty-one Saṅkhāras, viz:—

1. Phassa.
2. Cetanā.
3. Vitakka.
4. Vicāra
5. Pīti.
6. Viriya.
7. Jīvita.
8. Samādhi
9. Saddhā.
10. Sati.
11. Hiri.
12. Ottappa.
13. Alobha.
14. Adosa.
15. Amoha.
16. Kāyapassaddhi.
17. Cittapassaddhi.
18. Kāyalahutā.
19. Cittalahutā.
20. Kāyamudutā.
21. Cittamudutā.
22. Kāyakammaññatā.
23. Cittakammaññatā.
24. Kāyapāguññatā.
25. Cittapāguññatā.
26. Kāyujukatā.
27. Cittujukatā.
28. Chanda.

[1] Compendium of Philosophy, p. 274.

[2] Compendium of Philosophy, p. 276.

[3] Manual of Indian Buddhism, p. 52.

29. Adhimokkha.
30. Manasikāra.
31. Tatramajjhattatā.
32. Karuṇā.
33. Muditā.
34. Kāyaduccaritavirati.
35. Vacīduccaritavirati.
36. Micchājīvavirati.
37. Ahirika.
38. Anottappa.
39. Lobha.
40. Moha.
41. Micchādiṭṭhi.
42. Uddhacca.
43 and 44. Thīnamiddha.
45. Māna.
46. Dosa.
47. Issā.
48. Macchariya.
49. Kukkucca.
50. Cittaṭṭhiti.
51. Vicikicchā.

Khandha. There are five khandhas—Rūpakkhandha, Vedanākkhandha, Saññākkhandha, Saṅkhārakkhandha, and Viññānakhandha.

Rūpakkhandha is sub-divided into :—

A. Bhutarupa which includes—Paṭhavidhatu, Āpod hātu, Tejodhātu, and Vāyodhātu.

B. Upāḍārūpa which includes—Cakkhu, Sota, Ghāna, Jivhā, Kāya, Rūpa, Sadda, Gandha, Rasa, Itthindriya, Purisindriya, Jīvitindriya, Hadayavatthu, Kāyaviññatti, Vacīviññatti, Ākāsadhātu, Rūpassalahutā, Rūpassamudutā, Rūpassakammaññatā, Rūpassaupacaya, Rūpassasantati, Rūpassajaratā, Rūpassaaniccatā, Kabaḷiṅkāra āhāra.

Rūpakkhandha is of five kinds. For a detailed account of these kinds of Rūpakkhanda, see H. C. Warren's Table of Contents of Buddhaghosa's Visuddhimagga (J.P.T.S., 1891–3), pp. 124–5.

Kamma.

Buddha as a psychologist was quite content with the definition of Kamma as volition. Buddhaghosa framed a definition accordingly.[1] ("Cetanā 'haṁ, bhikkhave, kammaṁ vadāmi.") It appears from his explanation that an action is no action until the will is manifested in conduct, which goes to prove that his point of view is juristic or practical. Kamma means consciousness of good and bad, merit and demerit (kammaṁ nāma kusalākusala cetanā).[2] Kamma is of four kinds, diṭṭhadhammavedaniyaṁ, i.e. Kamma which produces result in this life; Upapaccavedaniyaṁ, i.e. Kamma which produces result in the next life; Aparāpariyāyavedaniyaṁ, i.e. Karma which produces result from time to time;[3] Ahosi Kamma, i.e. past Kamma.

We have another fourfold division of Kamma:—

1. Garukaṁ, i.e. an act be it good or bad which has a serious result.
2. Bahulaṁ, i.e. excess of either virtue or vice which produces its respective results.
3. Āsannaṁ, i.e. karma which is thought of at the time of death.
4. The Kaṭattā-Kammaṁ, i.e. an act which has been frequently done by one (in his life-time) and which in the absence of the three previous kammas, causes re-birth.

We have still another classification of Kamma:—

1. Janaka.
2. Upatthaṁbhako.

---

[1] Atthasālinī, p. 88 foll. [2] Visuddhimagga, Vol. II, p. 614. [3] Ibid., p. 601.

3. Upapīḷaka.
4. Upaghātako.

These twelve kinds of acts and their consequences are manifested in their true aspect in the Buddha's knowledge of the consequences of Kammas. These are not common to pupils; those who are endowed with spiritual insight come to know some of Kammantara and Vipākantara (Visuddhimagga, Vol. II, p. 602). Kamma produces consequence, retribution is born of action, action is the cause of re-birth, in this way the world continues. There is no originator of Kamma, no sufferer of consequences, only phenomena continue (Kammassa kārako natthi..... Visuddhimagga, Vol. II, p. 602). Kamma has its own individuality, has its own kinsman. It has its origin, has its friend. One will have to share the fruits of his Kamma be they good or bad (Visuddhimagga, Vol. II, p. 601). No action passes from the past life to the present nor from the present to the future (Visuddhimagga, Vol. II, p. 603).

Regarding the relation between kamma and vipāka, Buddhaghosa says that there is no kamma in vipāka and no vipaka in kamma. Each of them by itself is void, at the same time there is no vipāka without kamma. Just as there is no fire in the sun nor in the lense nor in the (dried) cow-dung and likewise fire is not outside them but comes into existence on account of these requisites, in the same way vipāka is not seen within the kamma nor it is outside the kamma. A kamma is void of its vipāka which comes through kamma. Vipāka comes into origin on account of kamma (Visuddhimagga, Vol. II, p. 603).

In the past, the khandhas, which originated as the consequences of action (volition), ceased. In this existence, other khandhas arise out of the consequences of past deeds, there is no condition which has come to this existence from the past, in this existence the khandhas which are originated on account of the consequences of kamma, are destroyed. In another existence, others will be produced from this existence, not a single condition will follow re-birth (Visuddhimagga, Vol. II, p. 603).

According to the Atthasālinī, kamma is of three kinds, kāyakamma, vacikamma and manokamma. It is cetanā and the states associated with it (p. 88). Childers in his Pāli Dictionary says, "All three originate in cetanā or the will." He further points out that kamma under the name of saṅkhāra is one of the links of Paṭiccasamuppāda (p. 176).

Buddhaghosa divides kamma into :—

1. Kammasamuṭṭānaṁ.
2. Kammapaccayaṁ.
3. Kammapaccayacittasamuṭṭhānaṁ.
4. Kammapaccaya-āhārasamuṭṭhānaṁ.
5. Kammapaccaya-utu-samuṭṭhānaṁ.

It is stated in the Kathāvatthupakaraṇa-aṭṭhakathā that there is a relationship between citta and kamma. If mind be distracted, no kamma can be performed. ("Yadā cittaṁ bhajjamānaṁ hoti tadā kammaṁ bhajjamānaṁ hotīti attho."[1]) Ledi Sadaw in his paper on the Philosophy of Relations (published in the J.P.T.S., 1915–16, p. 42), says, "Karma is ultimately reduced to the psychological

[1] J.P.T.S., 1889, p. 156.

factor of volition. And volition is the unique determination of will. Will-exercise is power over its co-existent mental properties and physical qualities. In fact, all our activities in deed, word, or thought are due to its influence. But here we are not concerned with the aspect of will in its relation to effects in after-life."

Childers says that as a religious technical term, the doctrine of kamma or the efficacy of good and bad works, is inseparably bound up with that of transmigration or renewed existence.[1] Undoubtedly kamma is one of the links of the Paṭiccasamuppāda. Old karma is destroyed and no new karma is produced ("khīnaṁ purāṇaṁ navaṁ n'atthi sambhavaṁ"). "Kammanā vattati loko, kammanā vattati pajā," the world exists through kamma and the people live through kamma.

Avijjā (Ignorance).

"Puretum ajuṭṭhena kāyaduccaritādi avindiyaṁ nāma, aladdhabban ti attho. Taṁ avindiyaṁ vindatīti avijjā." According to Buddhaghosa, avijjā means obtaining of that which is not to be obtained, namely, bodily sin, etc.

Birth is due to continued existence, continued existence is due to attachment, attachment is produced by desire, desire is due to sensation, sensation is produced by contact, contact is due to the six sense-organs, the six sense-organs are due to nāmarūpa, nāma and rūpa are due to consciousness, consciousness is due to saṅkhāra which is produced by ignorance.[2]

Avijjā is the root of existence in this world and it

[1] Pāli Dictionary, p. 178.

[2] Visuddhimagga, p. 600.

includes death, old age, etc. It is the cause of all saṅkhāras in the sensual existence, the cause of arūpasaṅkhāras in the formless existence. Saṅkhāras owed their existence in the past and will owe their existence in future to Avijjā.[1] Avijjā is one of the Āsavas, of the Oghas, of the Yogas, etc. (Childers' Pāli Dictionary, p. 73).

Avijjā means absence of knowledge of the four truths or of the eight matters as we find in the Abhidhamma. We quote the following passage from the Abhidhamma:—

"Katamā avijjā? Dukkhe aññānaṁ....pe dukkhanirodhagāminiyā paṭipadāya aññānaṁ, pubbante aññānaṁ, aparante pubbāparante, idappaccayatā paṭiccasamuppannesu dhammesu aññānaṁ."

Mrs. Rhys Davids translates āyatana as sphere[2] but Childers in his Pāli Dictionary, translates it as organ of sense and object of sense.[3] The twelve āyatanas have been enumerated in the Visuddhimagga,[4] namely, cakkhu, rūpa, sota, sadda, ghāna gandha, jivhā, rasa, kāya, phoṭṭabba, mana and dhamma.

Āyatana.

It is stated in the Visuddhimagga that the five sense organs (namely, eye, ear, nose, tongue, and skin) along with the mind make up the saḷāyatanas. Phassa is due to the six āyatanas. Buddhaghosa says[5] that the sense-organs are due to kamma and it is kamma which differentiates them. Their differentiation is not due to different elements which

1 Visuddhimagga, pp. 522 foll.

2 A Buddhist Manual of Psychological Ethics, p. 26.

3 Pāli Dictionary, p. 75.

4 Visuddhimagga, Vol. II, p. 481.

5 Visuddhimagga, pp. 444-445.

according to the Vaiśeṣika philosophy, are the constituents of the sense-organs.

Puggala. According to the Buddhists, the individual has no real existence. It is only a sammuti. Buddhaghosa accepts this view. He says that on the existence of khandhas such as rūpa, etc., there is the usage 'evaṁnāma,' 'evaṁgotta.' Because of this usage, common consent and name, there is the Puggala.[1]

Nāmarūpa.—Buddhaghosa is of the opinion that the three khandhas, Vedanā, Saññā and Saṅkhāras are the nāmaṁ because they bend towards the object. Rūpa, according to him, is the aggregate of and the outcome of the four mahābhūtas. (Visuddhimagga, Vol. II, p. 558). Nāmarūpa is one kind because of its being the support of consciousness and because of its being the cause of kamma. It is of two kinds as it is with or without any object. It is of three kinds according as it is past, present or future. It is of four or five kinds according to the course it takes for rebirths in different stages of existence.[2] In the section on Rūpakkhandha, Buddhaghosa has divided Rūpa into two, namely, Bhūtarūpa and Upādārūpa. By Bhūtarūpa, the four great elements are implied and Upādārūpa, according to him, is of twenty-four kinds.[3]

"Name has a two-fold aspect—to wit, (1) name as determined by convention or usage and (2) name in its ultimate

---

[1] Kathāvatthupakaraṇa-aṭṭhakathā, J.P.T.S., pp. 33-35.

[2] Visuddhimagga, Vol. II, p. 529. "Nāmarūpaṁ viññāṇasannissayato kammapaccayato ca ekavidhaṁ sārammaṇānārammaṇato duvidhaṁ. Atītādito tividhaṁ. Yonigativasena catubbidhaṁ pañcavidhañ ca."

[3] Ibid., pp. 443-444.

meaning. (1) In saying 'person' we give a name not to the aggregates (of a living organism) but to our idea corresponding to the form or appearance presented by those aggregates. And this idea or concept of an appearance does not exist objectively (independently of mind). Hence in this 'name' neither the meaning nor the name itself has any real existence. Yet the great majority perceive and imagine, when they recognise the name that there actually is what is named self or soul or entity or person. And for this reason we term name 'conventional' when it is merely determined as a designation by popular usage. But when not resting upon mere customary usage, people consider those ultimates, the aggregates, as self, soul, entity, person, then they exceed the scope of customary usage."

(2) "In name, under its ultimate aspect we are considering ultimate phenomena which are entirely without external appearance, and which are only modes and changes and phases of process. There is no 'life' (or 'living soul,' jīvo) apart from what we call the two powers or faculties of material and psychical life (Dve nāma rūpajīvitindriyāni)." "Now a 'living soul' is generally perceived and ordinarily reckoned as 'some one living a week, a month, a year,' etc.; the essence of the living appearance is commonly considered to be the self; the essence of its continuity is considered to be the 'living soul.' But the two powers or faculties of life referred to above are but the vital (coefficients) of momentary phenomena only, not of a personal entity." According to the conventional truth, "a person exists," "self exists," whereas according to the ultimate truth,

"neither does a person exist nor a self, there are only phenomena." According to the former, "it is not untruthful to say that there is a personal entity"; whereas according to the latter, "to say 'there is no personal entity' is neither untruthful nor mere opinion." (Ledi Sadaw, 'Some points in Buddhist Doctrine,' J.P.T.S., 1913–14, pp. 124–129.)

Buddhaghosa's contribution to Buddhist Philosophy.

It was Buddhaghosa who developed and perfected the Buddhist system of thought. According to some, Buddhism which now prevails in Ceylon is virtually the religion as interpreted by Buddhaghosa. The explanation of the sacred texts, literary and philosophical, which has prevailed since his time, is really the explanation of Buddhaghosa and his school.

In the Tripitaka itself we do indeed find many of the concepts that Buddhaghosa deals with, but it is in the works of this great commentator that these concepts acquire definiteness and become clear and intelligible. It is probable that in his interpretation of philosophical ideas, as in his exegesis of the other parts of the Buddhist sacred literature, Buddhaghosa received substantial help from the accumulated thoughts and ideas of many centuries as contained in the great Aṭṭhakathās wherefrom he derived his materials. It is difficult, nay impossible, to find out with any exactitude, what was his personal contribution to the ancient stock of knowledge, but whatever that may have been, we have to be grateful to Thera Buddhaghosa whose labours have simplified much of what was complex and rendered intelligible what was abstruse and vague.

CHAPTER VIII

BUDDHAGHOSA'S INTERPRETATION OF BUDDHISM

Authorities followed by Buddhaghosa.

In his interpretation of Buddhism, Buddhaghosa, as an orthodox Buddhist, closely follows the Tripiṭakas and the Sinhalese commentaries. The only authority outside the canonical literature quoted by him besides the commentaries of his predecessors, is the Milinda Pañho. Here and there he indulges in metaphysical and philological speculations to support his interpretation of the doctrines. In his metaphysical and psychological speculations, he has in some places improved upon the old ideas, and his philosophy, though sometimes fanciful, is generally correct. He always believed in miracles and never doubted their possibility. We give below his ideas about some important points of Buddhism.

Sīla.

All the authorities on Buddhism assign a very high place to sīla which, according to them, is the foundation of all good qualities. Sīla means "habit" or "good conduct." According to the quotation cited by Buddhaghosa from the Paṭisaṁbhidāmagga, it is divided into four parts, Cetanā sīlaṁ, Cetasika sīlaṁ, Saṁvara sīlaṁ and Avitikkamo sīlaṁ. The thought of a person who abstains from killing, etc., is called Cetanā Sīla. Saṁvara Sīlam is of five kinds, viz. Pātimokkhasaṁvara, Satisaṁvara, Ñānasaṁvara, Khantisaṁvara and

Viriyasaṁvara. Sīla is described as that which pacifies the mind or prevents fickleness of mind. Its function is to destroy evil deeds. The effect of its observance is to bring about the purity of body, mind and speech. It is of three kinds, Hīna, Majjhima and Paṇita, and there are sub-divisions of these three. When the precepts are not properly observed, the sīla is said to become impure. The Visuddhimagga contains a description of the evil effects of the violation of sīla. This description consists of quotations by Buddhaghosa from various authorities.[1] It is interesting to note that in the Atthasālinī, sīla is used in the same sense as in the Visuddhimagga.

Sīla is broadly divided into two, cārittasīla (duties of performance) and vārittasīla (duties of avoidance). It includes the following:—

1. To abstain from taking life;
2. Not to take what is not given;
3. Sexual purity;
4. To abstain from false, abusive, slanderous or idle speech;
5. To abstain from intoxicating drink.

"Habitual morality is compared to the broad earth, on which, as their fulcrum or basis, all creatures move, stand or rest; and again, sīla is compared to the sources of the great rivers and the ocean, starting as rill and burn way up in the mountains, and ministering to an increasing scale of animal growth as they descend and wax deep and wide, till merged in the ocean."[2]

---

[1] Visuddhimagga, Vol. I, pp. 6-58.

[2] Mrs. Rhys Davids, Buddhism, p. 154.

The word, 'Indriya' is applied ordinarily to the five sense-organs but the Buddhists take it in a very wide sense. It means not only the sense-organs but also the moral potentialities, principles, functions, etc. Buddhaghosa defines 'indriya' as "sā assaddhiyassa abhibhavanato adhipatiyaṭṭhena indriyaṁ adhimokkhalakkhaṇe vā indaṭṭham kāretīti indriyaṁ." [1] (As the indriya controls that which is not to be believed and as it implies the exercise of lordship, therefore, it is called indriya or by the characteristic of determination, it is called indriya because it causes to perform the purpose of inda.) In the Visuddhimagga, p. 491, Buddhaghosa takes the word inda in the sense of the Buddha. ("Bhagavā hi sammāsaṁbuddho paramissariyabhāvato indo.")

Indriya.

Buddhaghosa [2] mentions the following twenty-two indriyas:—

1. Cakkhundriya or organ of the eye.
2. Sotindriya or organ of the ear.
3. Ghānindriya or organ of smell.
4. Jivhindriya or organ of the tongue.
5. Kāyindriya or organ of the body.
6. Manindriya or organ of the mind.
7. Itthindriya or female-organ.
8. Purisindriya or male-organ.
9. Jīvitindriya or vital force.
10. Sukhindriya or principle of happiness.
11. Dukkhindriya or principle of suffering.

---

[1] Atthasālinī (P.T.S.), p. 119.

[2] Visuddhimagga, Vol. II, Chap. XVI., Indriya-sacca-niddesa.

12. Somanassindriya or principle of delight.
13. Domanassindriya or principle of sorrow.
14. Upekkindriya or principle of indifference.
15. Saddhindriya or principle of faith.
16. Viriyindriya or principle of energy.
17. Satindriya or principle of recollection.
18. Samādhindriya or principle of meditation.
19. Paññindriya or principle of wisdom.
20. Anaññātaññassāmītindriya or principle of knowing the unknown.
21. Aññindriya or principle of knowledge.
22. Aññātāvindriya or "sense of having thoroughly known."

"Indriya literally means 'a controlling principle or force.' The indriyas are the exercisers, the performers of lordship called sovereignty over this and that function..... The five (sense-organs), eye, etc., are lords of sight, etc., in the functions of seeing, etc."

"Cakkhundriyaṁ is not Cakkussaindriyaṁ, the 'power of the eye' but cakkhuṁ eva indriyaṁ, 'the eye which is a power.' The term has been rendered 'faculty of sight.' But we are not here speaking of the sense of sight, but of the eye itself, as exercising a certain control over the senses of sight."[1]

Piti. In the Visuddhimagga, Chapter IV, we find that Pīti is of five kinds:—

[1] Compendium of Philosophy, p. 229.

1. Khuddikā.
2. Khaṇikā.
3. Okkantikā.
4. Ubbegā.
5. Pharaṇā.

Of these Khuddikā Pīti is explained by Buddhaghosa to be that slight sense of interest which causes only the hairs of the body to stand on their ends; Khaṇikā Pīti appears like momentary flashes of lightning; Okkantikā Pīti is a deeper emotion that overfloods the body like waves sweeping over the sea-beach. Ubbegā Pīti is very strong and it causes the body to go up into the sky; Pharaṇā Pīti pervades the whole body like a great flood filling up a mountain cavern. (Atthasālinī, pp. 115–117.)

"There was, of course, at first a dull or slight sense of interest (Khuddakā Pīti) growing keener and keener through oscillating interest (Okkantikā Pīti) into an intense interest amounting to thrilling emotion (Ubbegā Pīti) followed finally by interest amounting to rapture (Pharaṇā Pīti). This diffused rapture is invariably followed by pleasurable, easeful, happy feeling (sukha) by which distraction and worry (uddhacca-kukkucca) are inhibited."[1] "Pīti has as its invariable concomitant somanassa, with which joy fits well enough, since the Pāli term means pleasure (sukha) plus excitement. But Pīti abstracted means interest of varying degrees of intensity, in an object felt as desirable or as calculated to bring happiness......... (Pīti is not hedonic but intellectual, having reference to an object in consciousness.....)

[1] Compendium of Philosophy, p. 56.

Pīti must not be misunderstood to mean a complex phenomenon. Even when present in the sublimated form of a bojjhaṅga or wisdom factor, it is still a factor or element, a simple element in a complex."[1]

It will be interesting to quote the following remarks of Mrs. Rhys Davids, "........if pīti be not bare feeling, it is unmistakably emotion. 'Emotional' is, has to be, used as the adjective of feeling. And Pīti is classed, not with feeling (vedanākkhandha), but among the co-efficients of consciousness called saṅkhāras or chetasikas. It is not simply pleasurable feeling (sukha). But neither is emotion to be so defined. Emotion is feeling accompanying an idea, the being 'moved' with a co-efficient of representative consciousness. The canonical description of Pīti allies it with terms of gladness, mirth and enthusiasm. Buddhaghosa gives, as its essential features, the being pleased, expansion and elation. He also gives us the five grades of Pīti: the thrill of eagerness, the momentary flash, the flood of enthusiasm, as waves breaking over us, ecstasy or transport, and rapture. And all the instances given refer to an idea or group of ideas as the proximate cause. Hence whereas no one word need suffice, 'joy' as the more exultant, uplifted form of interest or zest is by no means always a mistranslation."[2]

Buddhaghosa gives the following derivation of the word 'Upekkhā': Upapattito ikkhati, i.e. looks at from the very origination. He

Upekkhā.

[1] Compendium of Philosophy, pp. 243–244.

[2] Buddhist Psychology, Quest Series, pp. 187–188.

further says that the word implies 'looking equally and looking without being partial.' Upekkhā (indifference) is of ten kinds (dasavidhā) :—

1. Chalaṅga (six senses).
2. Brahmavihāra.
3. Bojjhaṅga (factor of wisdom).
4. Viriya (energy).
5. Saṅkhāra (aggregate).
6. Vedanā (sensation).
7. Vipassanā (insight).
8. Tatramajjhattā (balance of mind).
9. Jhāna (meditation).
10. Pārisuddhi (purification).[1]

The Abhidhammatthasaṅgaha mentions "three principal kinds of upekkhā. First, the anubhavana upekkhā (U of sensation or physical sensibility) : the neutral feeling or zero point between bodily pain and pleasure (kāyika-dukkha-sukha). This kind of upekkhā is applicable to all sensory stimuli, except those of touch. The second kind is the indriyappabhedaupekkhā or upekkhā dividing the (ethically) regulative forces of somanassa or joy and domanassa or grief (or of mental pleasure and pain)."

"Of these two kinds of upekkhā, the former is sensational, the latter is emotional, and both are hedonic."

"Lastly there is a third class of upekkhā, and that is a cetasika, of the nineteen sobhana-cetasikā ; in other words, a mental property or element, of the nineteen 'morally beautiful' properties."[2]

---

[1] Visuddhimagga, Vol. I, p. 160. [2] Compendium of Philosophy, pp. 229–230.

Samādhi.

Buddhaghosa describes samādhi as 'kusalacitte ekaggatā' or concentration of good thought. It is called samādhi because at the samādhi, all the thoughts are simultaneously and rightly centred on a particular object. Its characteristic is absence of distraction, its essence is the destruction of distraction, its immediate cause is firmness and its remote cause is happiness. Samādhi has been variously divided according to its predominant characteristics. Regarding the purity and impurity of samādhi, Buddhaghosa says that the condition which leads to its excellence, causes its purity while that which causes deterioration, brings about its impurity. Regarding the question of the practice of samādhi, Buddhaghosa says that there are two ways of practising it, lokiya and lokuttara. The practice of lokuttara-samādhi is but the culture of wisdom. The practice of lokiya-samādhi consists in purifying one's conduct, establishing oneself in the purified conduct, destroying the ten obstacles, adopting the practice of one of the forty Kammaṭṭhānas favourable to his mode of living, avoiding living in a manner unsuitable to the practice of meditation, destroying the minor impediments and applying oneself to the full observance of meditation. The advantages of practising meditation are the five kinds of happy living such as happy living in this world, insight, knowledge, re-birth in higher regions, and cessation.[1] The five blessings of samādhi are these :—

1. Diṭṭhadhamma-sukhavihāra (happy living in this world).

[1] Visuddhimagga, Vol. I, p. 84, foll.

2. Vipassanā (insight).
3. Abhiññā (intuitive knowledge).
4. Bhavavisesa (particular birth).
5. Nirodha (cessation).

" Samādhi means the placing, establishing of consciousness exclusively and voluntarily on any single object."[1] Mrs. Rhys Davids means by samādhi 'rapt concentration,'[2] 'concentrative meditation.'[3] She also speaks of it thus: "But the emphasis in samādhi is that of concentration, of an intensive attention, which can only be got by throwing overboard, into the sea of things disregarded and negligible, everything that is irrelevant and distracting to the single apex of thought (chitt'ekaggatā), which is the equivalent term to samādhi." [4]

There are ten hindrances of samādhi, viz :—

1. Āvāsa (dwelling place).
2. Kulaṁ (family).
3. Lābha (gain).
4. Gaṇa (assembly or congregation).
5. Kamma (work).
6. Addhānaṁ (walking along the street).
7. Ñāti (relation).
8. Āvāda (sickness).
9. Gantho (study).
10. Iddhi (miracle).

---

[1] Points of Controversy, p. 260, f.n. 3.

[2] Mrs. Rhys Davids, Buddhist Psychology, (Quest Series) p. 94.

[3] Ibid., p. 104. [4] Ibid., p. 105.

Jhāna.

Ordinarily the Jhānas or mystic meditations are considered to be of four kinds. In the first stage of meditation, five elements, viz:—Vitakkavicārapītisukha and ekaggatā, are present, in the second stage, the first two are eliminated, in the third, the first three are eliminated leaving sukham and ekaggatā. In the fourth, sukham is replaced by upekkhā and there are two elements, viz: upekkhā and ekaggatā. In his Visuddhimagga (Vol. I, pp. 168–169) Buddhaghosa speaks of five Jhanas. There is not much difference between these two sets of meditations. In the second stage of the first set of meditations, two elements, viz: vitakka and vicāra, disappear together but in the second set of meditations, they disappear one after another, thus giving opportunity for another stage. The third, fourth and fifth stage of the second set of meditations corresponds to the second, third and fourth stage of the first set.

With regard to Jhāna, five vasīs (powers) are to be obtained:—

1. Āvajjanavası (power of meditation).
2. Samāpajjanavasī (power of attainment).
3. Adhiṭṭhānavasī (power of resolution).
4. Vuṭṭhānavasī (power of exertion).
5. Paccavekkhanavasī (power of contemplation).[1]

Jhāna means 'contemplation.'[2] Mrs. Rhys Davids says, "And in the words Jhāna, contemplation, and samādhi, rapt concentration, are contained the expression of that

[1] Visuddhimagga, Vol. I, p. 154.

[2] Buddhist Psychology (Quest Series), p. 94.

self-training in selective, intensive work of mind in which the Indian sought, by changing the usual conditions and procedure in cognition, to induce consciousness of a higher or different power."[1]

Mrs. Rhys Davids further says that Jhāna or "ecstatic musing" was a practice prevalent from a long time similar to Yoga of the Hindus.[2] In her opinion "the more usual process of systematic elimination of factors in consciousness was that known as the four Jhānas."[3]

Vimuttiñānaṁ.

In the opinion of Buddhaghosa, Vimuttiñānaṁ (knowledge of emancipation) consists of knowledge of the following:—

Vipassanā (insight), magga (path), phala (fruition) and paccavekkhanaṁ (introspection). Of these, knowledge of insight is the knowledge of emancipation in as much as it is freed from the idea of the eternal character of things. By magga is meant the salvation due to destruction (of sin). Phala means emancipation due to equanimity and paccavekkhana means knowledge of emancipation.[4] The five vimuttis are these:—Tadaṅga (emancipation from its accompaniment), Vikkhaṁbhana (obstructing), samuccheda (uprooting), paṭipassaddhi (equanimity) and nissaraṇa (coming out).

Dhamma.

Buddhaghosa divides dhamma into guṇa, desanā, pariyatti and nissatta. He calls the three khandhas vedanā, saññā and saṅkhāra

[1] Buddhist Psychology (Quest Series), pp. 94–95. [2] Ibid, p. 107.

[3] Buddhist Psychology, p. 107.

[4] Kathāvatthupakaraṇa-aṭṭhakathā, p. 80.

nissattadhammā as well as nijjīvadhammā. (Dhammapada Aṭṭhakathā, Vol. I, p. 22).

The word dhamma, according to him, has a very wide application. It is in the last sense (i.e. nissattadhamma) of the word that it has been dealt with in the Atthasālinī.

Buddhaghosa following the Dhammasaṅgaṇi divides dhamma into kusala, akusala and avyākata. Kusala dhamma means the condition which is associated with pleasing sensation, akusala dhamma means the condition which is associated with painful sensation, and avyākata dhamma means the condition which is associated with sensation which is neither pleasing nor painful.[1]

Mrs. Rhys Davids says, "Dhamma implies that view or procedure which is, as we say, according to conscience, and constituting a more or less recognised standard, guiding rule, or norm." "Every religious or ethical teacher of ancient India had some 'Dhamma' to propound."[2] Dhamma has been translated as "the ideal, truth, law, right, system, or doctrine according to the context." Mrs. Rhys Davids further remarks, "But if Dhamma is a term common to Indian thought, Abhidhamma seems to be a term exclusively used by Buddhists. And for them, Abhidhamma, meaning literally beyond, or ultra dhamma, covers all study of theory as such, and of logical method."[3]

The difference between Dhamma and Abhidhamma is

---

[1] Atthasālinī, p. 36. [2] Buddhism, pp. 32–33.

[3] Buddhism, p. 36.

"Sukhāya vedanāya sampayuttā dhammā, dukkhāya vedanāya sampayuttā dhammā, adukkham-asukhāya vedanāya sampayuttā dhammā."

one of degree. Mrs. Rhys Davids quotes the opinion of Buddhaghosa regarding Abhidhamma thus, "It was calculated to check those excesses in thought away from the norm, which were shown, by the Buddha, to lead to loss of mental balance, craziness, insanity."[1]

Dhutaṅga.

Dhutaṅga means thirteen ascetic practices which are observed for acquiring special merit. Buddha said that these austerities might be observed but that there were no hard and fast rules for the performance of them. Buddhaghosa in his Visuddhimagga[2] gives an account of how these austerities can be observed. For those who have much enjoyed the world and do not take care of their body and soul, thirteen dhutaṅgas have been prescribed by the Buddha, namely—(1) putting on a robe made of rags collected from cemeteries, burning ghats or dust bins or garbages; (2) putting on only three robes; (3) living on alms only; (4) house-to-house begging; (5) eating food sitting once on one seat; (6) eating food from the alms-bowl; (7) eating food once received; (8) living in the forest; (9) living at the foot of trees; (10) living in an open space; (11) living in a cemetery; (12) being satisfied with whatever bedding one would get; (13) without lying down, passing one's days, sitting or walking, etc.

Nirvana.

Nirvāṇa, according to the Visuddhimagga,[3] is the cessation of five khandhas. The Visuddhimagga[4] says, 'ekaṁ hi saccaṁ na duti-

[1] Buddhism, p. 39.
[2] P.T.S., pp. 59–83.
[3] Pañcannaṁ khandhānaṁ nirodho, Vol. II, p. 611.
[4] Vol. II, p. 497.

yaṁ'—there is only one truth and no second. This is the idea of Nirvāṇa involved in this passage. Nirvāṇa includes absence of passion, destruction of pride, killing of thirst, freedom from attachment, destruction of all sensual pleasures. These are the attributes of Nirvāṇa.[1]

In the Nidānādikathā of the Visuddhimagga, we find that Nirvāṇa can be attained through meditation (jhāna), wisdom (paññā), precept (sīla), steadfastness[2] (āraddhaviriya), etc. As a man who has taken poison, asks for an antidote, so does a saint affected with the poison of worldly life, pray for the nectar-like medicine, Nirvāṇa.[3] Being bent upon self-concentration and Nirvāṇa (perfect beatitude), one should proceed towards salvation. In the Atthasālinī, Nirvāṇa means that from which the arrow of desire is gone away. It is freedom from all sins, "final release from the lower nature" as Mr. Maung Tin puts it.[4]

In the Sumaṅgalavilāsinī, we find that a person obtains Nirvāṇa which is immortality, making himself free from the wilderness of misdeeds. Nirvāṇa is described here as a state of bliss.[5] This is in agreement with what has been said of Nirvāṇa in the Milinda Pañho, p. 69.

---

[1] Visuddhimagga, Vol. I, p. 293.

[2] Ibid., Vol. I, p. 3.

[3] Ibid., Vol. II, p. 666.

"Yathā ca visasaṁphuṭṭho puriso visaghātanaṁ bhesajjaṁ pattheti, evaṁev' āyaṁ kilesavisasamphuṭṭho yogāvacaro kilesavisanimmathanaṁ amatosadhaṁ Nibbānaṁ pattheti."

[4] Atthasālinī, p. 409. Expositor, Vol. II., p. 518.

"Taṇhāsaṅkhātaṁ vānaṁ niggataṁ vā tasmā vānā ti nibbāṇaṁ."

[5] Sumaṅgalavilāsinī, Vol. I, p. 217.

"duccarita-kantāraṁ nittharitvā paramaṁ khemanta-bhūmiṁ Amata-Nibbānaṁ pāpuṇāti."

Elsewhere, Buddhaghosa describes Nirvāṇa as a void.[1] This appears to be contradictory but this apparent contradiction can easily be removed if we take into consideration the fact that the Buddhists believed in two different stages of Nirvāṇa. One they used to call the Savupādisesanibbāṇa and the other, Anupādisesanibbāṇa. The first is reached with the attainment of Arahatship and the second after death. The first is a blissful state and the second is a void inasmuch as it means complete cessation of existence. So Buddhaghosa when he speaks of Nirvāṇa as a blissful existence, refers to the state of an Arahat and when he speaks of it as a void, he evidently means the second stage of Nirvāṇa or complete cessation of existence.

Buddhaghosa explains Parinibbāṇa as a state which a person acquires after removing all fetters (saṁyojanaṁ).[2]

Mrs. Rhys Davids speaks of Nibbāṇa thus, "Nibbāṇa is the realization of the final culminating stage in a single stream of life evolving from eternity."[3] We quite agree with the learned author when she says that Nibbāṇa is a quasi-negative term which "was at times employed as health, as well as happiness."[4]

---

[1] Kathāvatthupakaraṇa-aṭṭhakathā, J.P T S., 1889, p. 178, cf. Dhammapada, Verse 93.

"Yassāsavā parikkhīnā, āhāre ca anissito, | suññato animitto ca vimokho yassa gocaro, | ākāse va sakuntānaṁ padaṁ tassa durannayam."

[2] Kathāvatthupakaraṇa-aṭṭhakathā, p. 193.

[3] Buddhism, p. 170.

[4] Buddhist Psychology (Quest Series), p. 82.

CONCLUSION

In the foregoing pages we have made an attempt to present an account of the life and work of the great Buddhist commentator Buddhaghosa. The quality and bulk of the work produced in a single life-time show that our author must have been toiling steadily and indefatigably, year in and year out, working out the mission with which he was entrusted by his teacher, immured in a cell of the great monastery at Anurādhapura. Such a life is necessarily devoid of events, and we cannot expect to find in it the variety and fulness of the life-story of a great political figure. We have to be satisfied here with the bits and fragments that can be gathered from the great works that form the best record of the life of the great commentator. The long distance of centuries that separates us from his own times, has made the work of ascertaining the authentic events of his career a task of particular difficulty. Often we run the risk of being carried away by the enthusiasm of the biographer and take for actual history what was but fiction. However, a few facts of undoubted authenticity come out from this mixture of romance and history, of fanciful invention and authentic tradition, and tested in the light of references in the works left behind by the author himself, they give us an account that may be taken as genuine, though scanty and meagre, and at the conclusion of our work, we think we can do no better than take stock of these few events about which perhaps there can be no doubt.

Born in northern India, Buddhaghosa was brought up in the Brahmanic traditions. He had a wide knowledge of Indian literature, including the sacred lore of the Brahmins and works on both science and art. He mastered the three Pitakas and studied the Sinhalese commentaries. He was conversant with the system of Patañjali and was apparently himself a follower of the system before he embraced the Buddhist faith. Not only the Yoga but Sāṅkhya system was also known to him, as is apparent from his works. These, moreover, abound in references to the canonical literature as contained in the Piṭakas, the Sinhalese commentaries, the Milinda-Pañho, the Peṭaka and so on. The commentator has thoroughly studied the Abhidhamma literature from which he drew a good deal of his materials. His art of handling difficult philosophical problems is masterly, as is manifested in erudite works like the Atthasālinī and the Kathāvatthupakaraṇa-aṭṭhakathā. He studied Buddhism thoroughly and he dealt with the subject carefully in his Visuddhimagga which is a vast treasure-house of Buddhist lore. He enriched the Buddhist literature by drawing new materials from other sources. He studied the history of Ceylon thoroughly; he often refers to the Ceylonese kings, districts, vihāras, etc., in his works, notably in his Visuddhimagga and the Dhammapada-aṭṭhakathā. He was undoubtedly one of the great celebrities of the Mahāvihāra at Anurādhapura. He is rightly regarded as a great teacher of mankind. Mahayanism, however, does not appear to have been studied by him. Nowhere in his works does he make any mention of it.

James Gray is perfectly right in saying, "Buddhaghosa stands out as a grand figure in the annals of Buddhism." He not only praises the commentator as a commentator but also his commentaries. He says, "the colossal nature of the work accomplished by him as a translator and expounder of Buddha's words, the profound scholarship brought to bear upon that work, and the almost superhuman zeal and self-denial manifested by him to execute it, evoke the highest esteem and admiration on the part of those who have made Pāli literature a study" .... (Buddhaghosuppatti, Introduction, p. 1.)

Mrs. Rhys Davids says that Buddhaghosa apparently resembled the European philosophers prior to Hume and Hartley so far as the problems of representative cognition or of the association of ideas are concerned—"for Spinoza's statements (Ethics, II. XVII, XVIII) carry us no further than Buddhaghosa's as psychological theory though they are better summaries." (Buddhist Psychology, p. 191.)

Bishop Copleston in his work on Buddhism (Primitive and Present) says, "It would be hardly too much to say that Buddhaghosa was the second founder of Buddhism of Ceylon" (p. 201). He was called the second founder of Buddhism in Ceylon because he came there after Mahinda. Kern speaks of him as "the most celebrated of southern Buddhist authors."[1]

Almost all European scholars give their best compliments to Buddhaghosa as a commentator. It seems really

---

[1] Manual of Indian Buddhism by H. Kern, p. 125.

surprising that although he was at first brought up in brahmin traditions and was an adherent of the system of Patañjali, he acquired such a thorough mastery over the Pāli language and literature that it enabled him to read and appreciate the Pāli Piṭakas and perform his task so ably later on.

His was a useful career. Although it is not definitely known when he died, it is conceivable that he lived long to see his labours amply rewarded and to enjoy the wide fame that he so well deserved.

As long as Buddhism remains a living faith among mankind, Buddhaghosa will not cease to be remembered with reverence and gratitude by Buddhist peoples and schools.

It is a pity that an opinion is being propounded in some quarters that Buddhaghosa is not a historical personage, that he did not live and write the many works that bear his name. Mrs. Rhys Davids in her learned Foreword to this work, points out that a hypothesis of this nature has been lately put forward by M. L. Finot.[1] We shall consider ourselves amply rewarded if the foregoing sketch of the life and career of the great Buddhist author, serves to convince our readers that he was a real person who lived and worked for the propagation of the Buddhist faith and for the interpretation of the Buddhist literature.

[1] See La Légende De Buddhaghosa. Cinquantenaire De L'Ecole Pratique des Hautes Etudes, Paris, 1921. It is a pamphlet of 19 pages written in French on the legends of Buddhaghosa, so kindly presented to me by M. Louis Finot. We regret that we cannot agree with him in his views. We fully concur with Mr. Pe Maung Tin in all that he says in his critical review of this paper in J.R.A.S., April, 1923, pp. 265–269.

INDEX